To Root & To Rise

ACCEPTING BRAIN INJURY

Carole J. Starr, M.S.

Spiral Path Publishing
Cape Elizabeth, Maine

Spiral Path Publishing
www.spiralpathpublishing.com

Book Layout ©2013 BookDesignTemplates.com

Cover Design by Kristofor Shisler & Carole J. Starr
Image Credits: Tree: rolandtopor/shutterstock.com, Bird: Rimma Kovalenko/shutterstock.com

Ordering Information: Special discounts are available on quantity purchases by corporations, associations, and others. For details, contact the publisher at the website above.

To Root & To Rise/ Carole J. Starr —1st ed.
ISBN 978-0-9986521-0-8
Library of Congress Control Number: 2017906106

Disclaimer: This book details the author's personal experience accepting brain injury. The author is not a medical or mental health professional. This book is not a substitute for health advice from a qualified professional. Readers should consult their own practitioners.

Table of Contents

To my mother, Joyce Starr, and my mentor, Bev Bryant:
Your influence lives on.

To all who share this brain injury path:
We journey together.

Happiness can exist only in acceptance.

~George Orwell

Preface

Uprooted

You never know when life is going to change so dramatically that it shakes the very ground you stand on. My life was uprooted on July 6th, 1999, when I sustained a brain injury in a car accident. That day forever divides my life into a before and an after, an old Carole and a new Carole.

On July 5th, 1999, the day before my accident, I was 32 years old. I was a daughter, a sister and a friend. I wanted to add wife and mother to that list. I think we all have identities that we especially cherish, that define who we are. For me, one of those identities was 'brain'. Above all else, I defined myself by my sharp intellect, quick wit and ability to achieve. I'd been the valedictorian of my high school class and graduated magna cum laude and third in my college class. I was proud of what I'd accomplished. I worked hard, but rarely struggled. I was accustomed to succeeding at most everything I did.

Two activities that brought great joy to my life were teaching and music. Teaching began for me all the way back in elementary school, when I tutored my classmates. No matter where I was, I always seemed to find myself in positions that involved teaching. After receiving my master's degree in Adult Education, I was primarily self-employed as a free-lance corporate trainer. I loved learning new material and figuring out creative ways to teach it.

Outside of work, I was very involved in classical music. I'd been a violinist for 23 years. I played in a community orchestra and I also sang in a chorus. I absolutely loved being a musician—rehearsing, performing, being surrounded by sound. Music gave me the opportunity to be part of something bigger than myself. It fed my soul in a way that nothing else did. Lots of people love loud rock music. I loved loud classical music. I planned to be an amateur musician for the rest of my life.

On July 6th, 1999, I was on my way from one teaching job to another when I was broadsided on the driver's side by a car going about 50 mph. The last thing I remember is the earsplitting sound of metal on metal. The airbags went off, the windows shattered and my car spun 180 degrees as it was being pushed across the road. I have no memory of any of those things, since I think I lost consciousness at the moment of impact. I only know they happened from the accident photos that I saw later on.

When I opened my eyes after the accident, the driver of the other car was already at my window, yelling 'Get out!', 'Get out!', 'Get out!' I wasn't really sure why or what was happening, but I complied. Because the driver's side door was completely crushed in and wouldn't open, I had to crawl out of the car through the passenger side. As I stood in the middle of the road, I felt dazed, confused and off-balance.

The midday light seemed especially bright. An off-duty paramedic stopped at the scene and led me to the median to lie down until the ambulance arrived.

I was transported to the emergency room by ambulance, a ride that I don't remember. At the hospital, my head hurt. However, I didn't know to share that information with the doctor. He also asked me if I remembered everything about the accident. I confidently answered yes, not realizing that my memory of the event actually had rather large holes in it. When asked if I'd lost consciousness, I said no. It didn't occur to me that in my recollection, the driver of the other car was at my window, yelling at me, instantly after the accident. In reality, I was probably unconscious during the time it took him to get out of his car and come over to mine. I was sent home from the emergency room with a diagnosis of severe whiplash and told I should be fine in a few weeks.

It was the physical therapist I saw for the whiplash who suspected I also had a brain injury. My primary care physician agreed that I'd had a mild traumatic brain injury and told me I should recover fully. He recommended gradually resuming my normal activities. I didn't really understand what mild traumatic brain injury meant, but I looked forward to getting back to my regular life as soon as possible. I figured the 'brain stuff' was minor. I was more focused on healing what I called the 'screaming pain' in my neck due to the whiplash.

As I tried to return to my regular life about 6 weeks after the accident, the impact of my brain injury became more apparent. The symptoms that were mostly hidden when I was resting a lot due to the whiplash suddenly became much more prominent and problematic.

I was utterly exhausted and my head hurt all the time. It felt like someone was squeezing the left side of my brain from the inside. Sometimes it felt like there was so much pressure in my head that it was going to explode right out the top.

While teaching, I suddenly couldn't remember my students' names, something I'd always been good at. Every time they came to class, I thought they were new, even though they'd been there each session. I would forget what topics we'd discussed and I lost track of what we were doing. I struggled to follow the lesson plan that I'd written and used many times before. It seemed like everyone was speaking too fast and I couldn't focus or follow the conversation. Often I'd put the students in groups to work and leave them there long after they'd finished the task, because I was so overwhelmed. After only two hours of teaching, I would spend two solid days just glued to my couch or bed, too exhausted to do anything at all. I could barely manage just four hours of work a week.

Even the simplest of activities would bring on the crushing mental fatigue. For example, I had to take a nap each day right after my morning shower because it tired me so much. I would be too wiped out to even use the hairdryer, so I would just collapse on the couch with my hair still wet. This led to many interesting hair days.

The fatigue was unlike anything I'd ever experienced in my life. At first, I blamed it on the pain medication I was still taking for the whiplash. But the symptoms continued even after I'd finished the medication.

I also tried to return to music. I'd played in orchestras since childhood, so that environment had always been like a second home. Not anymore. When I walked in while everyone was warming up, the

jumble of conversations and instrumental sounds instantly overwhelmed me. It seemed piercingly loud. The sound was everywhere
in my head. When I opened my violin case, I saw that one of my
strings had broken. I'd been changing strings for decades, but suddenly couldn't remember how to anymore. Even though I'd had the same
seat in that orchestra for nearly ten years, I didn't know where to sit.
Once the rehearsal started, I lasted about five minutes before the
sound reduced me to tears and I ran from the room. I couldn't remember how to get home, so a friend drove me. I spent days on my
couch recovering from just a few minutes of music. It seemed like the
ultimate cruel joke to curse a musician with an intolerance to sound.

I didn't know it then, but my brain injury had left me with
hyperacusis, an extreme sensitivity to sound. Every kind of noise
sounded louder to me than it really was. For example, whenever a
plane would go overhead, I would duck, because it sounded like it was
coming right at me. A sudden loud sound like an alarm would cause
me to scream, lose my balance, and sometimes fall.

I also struggled with basic life activities. At the grocery store, I would
stand in the produce section for long periods of time with an apple in
each hand, unable to figure out which one to put in the bag. Once I
spent half an hour in the bread aisle because they were out of the
brand I buy and I didn't know what to do. I ended up calling my
mother because I was so confused. The food I did buy would go bad
because I couldn't figure out what to do with it. For some strange
reason, I became fixated on cottage cheese and that was what I ate for
dinner most nights. I'd always loved to read, but I stopped reading the
paper and magazines and books because it was so hard to focus, pay
attention and remember what I'd read.

Family gatherings, which I'd always enjoyed, suddenly became unbearable. I had a hard time holding a conversation, especially if more than one person was talking or there was lots of background noise. I couldn't remember what people told me. I tried to hide just how little I was able to comprehend and remember. My speaking was slow and halting and I'd lose my words. Often I just didn't say anything.

I felt so alone, like a stranger among the people who knew me best. It was like I'd lost my place in my own family. As a grown-up, independent woman, I was embarrassed by how much assistance I needed from both my family and my friends. I often called them in tears because I was confused and unsure what to do. I desperately needed their help but often didn't want to accept it. I felt that I was a burden to everyone and a failure as an adult.

My emotions were no longer within my control. I overloaded and cried a lot—over the strangest of things. I sobbed hysterically during sappy commercials on TV, if plans changed unexpectedly and when a bumblebee flew into my house. I wondered if I was losing my mind.

I kept thinking that if I just tried harder or pushed more, I could make the symptoms go away by sheer force of will. I'd always been someone who believed that anything is possible if you just work hard enough. For the first time in my life, that was no longer true. The harder I pushed, the worse everything got. I felt like an absolute failure. I blamed myself for not trying hard enough, for being weak, for being lazy, when none of those judgments were true.

I tried over and over again to return to teaching and music, but each time I failed. Eventually, I had to stop both. My life was reduced to medical appointments and four naps a day. I'd become someone I didn't recognize anymore, someone I absolutely hated. 'The brain' was no longer an identity that described me. Every day was a struggle to function at a basic level.

As it became clear that the old Carole was gone and a new Carole had taken her place, the grief over all I'd lost was overwhelming. It was the most intense grief that I'd ever experienced, worse than grief from the loss of loved ones. This time it was me who had died. Even though I survived my car accident, I had lost my sense of self. I thought the grief was going to break me. There were numerous times when I thought seriously about ending my life.

It took me eight years and much help from family, friends, other brain injury survivors and medical professionals to come to terms with the new Carole. Accepting my life as a brain injury survivor was the greatest challenge I've ever faced. There were many, many times when I thought I couldn't do it. But I did learn to accept brain injury and to like myself again. I've gone from being uprooted by brain injury, to putting down new roots to rising into this changed life and finding a way to soar. My life is very different than I ever thought it would be, but it is again filled with meaning, purpose and joy.

There are many paths to acceptance. The strategies I've included in this book are ones that worked for me. I'm a brain injury survivor sharing what I've learned with other brain injury survivors. I'm not a medical or mental health professional. Please take whatever information is useful to you on your own brain injury journey and leave the rest behind.

Introduction

We do not learn from experience...
we learn from reflecting on experience.

~John Dewey

This book is a reflection on my experience as a brain injury survivor. I've spent a lot of time thinking deeply about my journey and how I can use what I've learned to help others living with brain injury. I didn't think I could ever accept this changed life, but I eventually did. Now I'm sharing the strategies that worked for me. I'd like this book to offer hope to others who are struggling to come to terms with brain injury. Reaching acceptance may not be easy, but it is possible.

Why Acceptance?

In my opinion, accepting brain injury and its impact on our lives is one of the most important tasks we face as survivors. It can also be one of the most difficult. When your life has been uprooted by brain injury symptoms and you don't recognize the person in the mirror anymore, acceptance of the new you can seem like an impossible task. It's hard to imagine that life after brain injury can ever be happy or purposeful.

It seems unlikely, but coming to acceptance can be a key that opens the door to happiness and purpose after brain injury. Even though acceptance doesn't change the reality or the challenge of brain injury symptoms, it can change how you experience those symptoms. Acceptance is like looking at the world through a different lens. Coming to terms with brain injury can mean the difference between a mournful life spent looking backward at what was and a meaningful life spent moving forward with what is.

Coming to acceptance is a process, a journey. The poems on the next two pages describe some of that journey. They're also the inspiration for the title of this book.

I wrote the first poem, *Phoenix*, about nine months after my brain injury, when fear and uncertainty about the future loomed large. I wrote the second poem, *Phoenix—Revisited*, about four years post-injury, when acceptance was just beginning to take root in me. Although I wrote these poems from a deeply personal place, it's my hope that they speak to you too, wherever you are in your own journey.

Phoenix

At the end
of my street,
on the edge
of the marsh,
stands a tree.

She does more than stand.
She commands
your attention,
full of her fall flash.
No ordinary red, orange and yellow for her.
She sparkles with crimson, magenta, umber & ocher plumage,
A rising phoenix with outstretched wings,
confident and bold.

But her time is brief.
Perhaps her colors burned too brightly.
Her plumage dulls,
darkens
and drops,
exposing frail, gray bones,
pale and naked.

Who
is she now?

The tree will have her time again.
Will I?

Phoenix—Revisited

At the end
of my street,
on the edge
of the marsh,
stands that same tree.

The haunting, hoping desire,
'The tree will have her time again.
Will I?'
finally answered with a quiet confidence—
No.

For that is the wrong question.
I am no longer that tree.
I am a new being, on a new journey,
spinning, sailing, falling, flailing, writhing, wailing,
Landing
in my own soft space.
Safe
to root and to rise,
to live,
this new time.

The Story of this Book

Reaching acceptance is a process; writing a book is too. I started working on this book about five years after my brain injury. At this writing in 2017, I'm approaching eighteen years as a survivor. It's taken me so long to complete this project for a couple reasons. First, my brain injury symptoms slowed the process down and increased the challenge. I'm no longer able to write and think quickly or consistently, so everything takes more time.

Second, and more important, I had to be ready to write this specific type of book. I knew from the start that I didn't want to tell my brain injury story beginning to end, in chronological order. There are already many excellent books out there that cover the brain injury survivor experience in that way. I wanted to write a different kind of book.

Because I've always been a teacher, I tend to think about everything in terms of learning and lessons. I like to look for the bigger picture and the meaning in experiences. I wanted to use my story as a vehicle to share what I'd learned as a brain injury survivor. I envisioned that each book chapter would be a different lesson or strategy. I wanted the final product to be a book of wisdom about living with brain injury.

During my first several years of writing, I produced many half-finished chapters. I knew I wanted to expand them beyond telling only my brain injury story, but I didn't have enough insight to do that yet. It takes many years in life to gain wisdom. Similarly, it takes many years of living with brain injury to be able to look back and see the bigger picture of that experience.

From 2010-2015, I didn't work on the book. I felt stuck and couldn't seem to turn my vision into reality. Instead, I focused on what I could do with my ten-plus years of experience as a brain injury survivor.

I co-founded the survivor education, advocacy and peer mentoring group Brain Injury Voices. I led workshops, advocated for brain injury issues, facilitated a support group and mentored other survivors. I wrote two keynote speeches on happiness and resilience and delivered them at brain injury conferences. My dream of writing a book didn't die, but it did recede into the background.

I didn't realize it at the time, but even though I wasn't working on this book, I was laying its groundwork. Through all those activities, I was learning how to look at my brain injury journey and see patterns in how it had unfolded.

At the end of 2015, I realized what the book needed—an overall theme to the individual chapters. In a big 'Aha!' moment, I knew that acceptance was that theme. There are times when life snaps into sudden focus. This was one of those times.

I realized that I wanted to help other survivors move toward acceptance. Because I'd struggled so much with acceptance before finding my own peace, I wanted to share what I'd learned. I also knew that I'd gained enough distance from my own acceptance journey to be able to see the patterns in it and to write about the process. I was finally ready to write the book I'd envisioned back in 2004. In 2016, I rededicated myself to writing the book and finished it in 2017.

The Structure of this Book

I've put the chapters of this book in an order that makes sense to me, based on my own brain injury acceptance journey. However, you don't have to read them in that order. Each chapter is a separate essay, not dependent on what comes before it. For example, you don't have to read chapters one and two in order to understand chapter three. I did that on purpose, so you can read this book in any order that makes sense to you. It's about whatever is most helpful for you, wherever you may be on your brain injury journey.

The chapters have also been designed with you, the brain injury survivor, in mind. Most of them are relatively short, since many of us struggle with reading and remembering long texts. The longer chapters have been divided into sections, so they can be processed one small chunk at a time. The font size is larger than average, to improve the readability for those with visual issues. There are also spaces between each paragraph, to reduce the overwhelmed feeling that can come from looking at too much text. I made these design decisions to make this book as readable as possible for brain injury survivors.

As survivors, each of us is on a journey that is uniquely ours. I hope that sharing my brain injury acceptance journey will help you navigate yours. Powerful learning can happen from reading about another survivor's experience.

However, when you can also think, write and talk about your own brain injury experience, the learning multiplies and becomes even more powerful. Therefore, in the spirit of learning by reflecting on experience, I've structured this book as a workbook.

The workbook format allows you to take my experience of accepting brain injury and make it your own. There are questions for thought or discussion in each chapter, as well as space to write your answers, if you choose to. The questions are designed to make you think about your experience. They're also a way for you to record your own brain injury acceptance journey.

Use the questions in whatever way works best for you. You can think and write about them on your own or discuss them with family, friends or medical professionals. You can also answer the questions in a group setting, such as a brain injury support group. Some of the ideas in this book may be challenging, so I encourage you to take whatever time and help you may need to work through them.

Let's begin the journey.

CHAPTER 1

Defining Acceptance

The world as we have created it is a product of our thinking.
It cannot be changed without changing our thinking.

~Albert Einstein

Acceptance is an abstract concept that's hard to define. What does accepting brain injury really mean? What does acceptance look like? How do you know when you've accepted your injury?

Acceptance is a term that gets thrown at brain injury survivors a lot. Perhaps you've heard statements like 'You have to accept what's happened to you' or 'It's time to accept your brain injury and move on'. Statements like that make it sound so easy. We all know it's incredibly difficult. The first step in moving toward acceptance is being clear about what it is. Let's start by defining it.

Acceptance is acknowledging the reality of a situation. It's about recognizing the difference between what can be changed and what can't. It's being able to say—without any internal resistance— 'It is what it is'.

There are many misconceptions about acceptance. When I first heard the word acceptance, here's what I thought about it:

- Acceptance means I have to give up on healing my brain.
- Acceptance means that where I am now is where I will always be.
- Acceptance means being resigned to the fact that brain injury has ruined my life forever.
- Acceptance means that I have to like having a brain injury and to welcome the symptoms into my life.

It turns out that my ideas about acceptance were wrong. Here's what I've learned about brain injury acceptance:

- Acceptance isn't a one-time event. It happens in many small pieces over time.
- Acceptance isn't agreeing with or liking what's happened to me. I can wish my brain injury never happened while still accepting the symptoms and their impact on me.
- Acceptance isn't giving up on making progress. It's letting go of trying to get back to the old me. It's about becoming the new me.
- Acceptance isn't the end of my brain injury symptoms, but it is the end of suffering emotionally when they affect my life.
- Acceptance is knowing that brain injury has changed me forever. I will deal with brain injury symptoms for the rest of my life.
- Acceptance is acknowledging my limitations—what I can and can't do—and working with them instead of fighting against them.
- Acceptance is recognizing when I need help and listening to advice from the people who know me best.

- Acceptance is letting go of what I can't control and focusing my energy on what I can control.
- Acceptance is being ok with where I am right now, even as I strive for more.
- Acceptance is focusing on what I <u>can</u> do.
- Acceptance is recognizing that even though my life is different than I thought it would be, it's not ruined. Life with a brain injury can still be good.
- Acceptance is a courageous choice I make for myself.

My favorite definition of acceptance comes from one of its synonyms: the word acquiescence. It's derived from the Latin word that means 'to take rest in'. We've reached acceptance when we've found our own place of peace, even as the storms of brain injury swirl all around us.

Defining acceptance is the beginning of the journey. Now that you know where we're going, it's time to focus on moving in that direction. The rest of this book is focused on strategies that can lead toward accepting brain injury.

Making it Your Own

Defining Acceptance

Have you had any of these misconceptions about acceptance?

- ☐ Acceptance means I have to give up on healing my brain.
- ☐ Acceptance means that where I am now is where I will always be.
- ☐ Acceptance means being resigned to the fact that brain injury has ruined my life forever.
- ☐ Acceptance means that I have to like having a brain injury and to welcome the symptoms into my life.

Which of these statements about brain injury acceptance stand out to you the most?

- ☐ Acceptance happens in many small pieces over time.
- ☐ Acceptance isn't agreeing with or liking what's happened to me.
- ☐ Acceptance isn't giving up on making progress.
- ☐ Acceptance is the end of suffering emotionally when brain injury symptoms affect my life.
- ☐ Acceptance is knowing that brain injury has changed me forever.
- ☐ Acceptance is acknowledging my limitations
- ☐ Acceptance is recognizing when I need help
- ☐ Acceptance is letting go of what I can't control and focusing my energy on what I can control.

☐ Acceptance is being ok with where I am right now, even as I strive for more.

☐ Acceptance is focusing on what I <u>can</u> do.

☐ Acceptance is recognizing that even though my life is different than I thought it would be, it's not ruined.

☐ Acceptance is a courageous choice I make for myself.

Taking it Further

What's one thing you learned from reading this chapter?

_____

_____

_____

What action are you ready to take?

_____

_____

_____

CHAPTER 2

The First Year: If I Knew Then What I Know Now

We have to do with the past only as we can make it useful to the present and the future.

~Frederick Douglass

The journey toward acceptance starts at the moment of one's brain injury. The road is often at its most rocky and steep during the early days, months and years, when everything is new and confusing.

A newspaper article inspired this chapter about the first year after brain injury. The article profiled a man who created a video in which he spliced together old footage of himself at age twelve with more recent footage of himself as a grown man. Through skillful editing, he made it look as if his adult self and his twelve-year old self were having a conversation.

As I read this story, it gave me an idea. As a now long-term survivor, if I could talk to my newly brain-injured self, what advice would I give her? What would I like to have known at a few key moments during that most challenging first year after brain injury? What knowledge would have helped me the most then? I've answered those questions in the form of three letters to myself—long-term survivor Carole writing to first-year survivor Carole. It's my hope that this hard-won wisdom will be useful to others who are struggling to cope with brain injury, especially during that bewildering first year post-injury.

Why Am I So Tired?

August 1999—Six Weeks after Brain Injury

Dear First-Year Survivor Carole,

You've just found out that the injuries you sustained in your July 6th car accident are more serious than whiplash, bumps and bruises. You have a traumatic brain injury. At this point, you have no idea what that means or how it will impact your life.

You're bewildered as to why you're so tired and overwhelmed all the time. You can't seem to sleep enough to get rid of the exhausted feeling. Your head hurts; it's a constant feeling of pressure on the left side that makes you feel dazed and confused. Your ears are so sensitive that two people talking at the same time sounds like a whole crowd. Noise quickly overwhelms your system and makes you feel dizzy and off-balance. You cry easily and often for no reason. You're confused a lot, but you're putting up a brave front and pretending to be better than you are. You're embarrassed at how much difficulty you're having doing formerly simple tasks, like reading, shopping and cooking.

You've been out of work for six weeks and you're now trying desperately and unsuccessfully to return to teaching and to your hobby of classical music performance. You know you're not right, but it's hard to pinpoint what's wrong.

It doesn't help that many people are telling you that you 'look great!' and saying 'oh that happens to me too' when you try and explain your difficulties. You're thinking that if you just try harder or push harder, all the symptoms will go away. You feel weak, like a failure, because this approach isn't working. You don't understand why you can't just snap out of the deep tiredness that's taken over your life.

As a long-term survivor, here's what I've learned that I'd like to share with you. *Fatigue after brain injury is completely different than fatigue before brain injury.* Needing to rest a lot doesn't mean you're weak, unmotivated or lazy. Brain injury fatigue doesn't respond to the usual fixes that used to work, such as a brief nap, a cup of coffee, or a quick walk around the block. The only thing that works is to lie down flat in a quiet, dark place and to rest as long as needed. Often that's hours or sometimes even days.

When the brain has been injured, it needs lots of extra rest, more than after other types of injuries. Tasks that were simple before, like thinking, talking, filtering out light and sound, and managing emotions, are all now difficult. They require a tremendous amount of mental energy. The injured brain runs out of steam, necessitating frequent, long-lasting rest periods.

It's pointless to try and push the injured brain when it's overtired. All that does is make the symptoms worse. To use the metaphor of a car, brain injury fatigue is like running out of gas. When your car runs out of gas, you can't argue with it—'you're not out of gas'. You also can't bargain with it—'if you give me an extra 10 miles, I'll fill you with premium'. All you can do is refill the tank. The same is true with regard to brain injury fatigue. Rest times are refueling and necessary to recharge the brain. They're not evidence of laziness. Listen to your brain and get the rest that you need.

With Love from your Future Self,

Carole
Long-Term Survivor Carole

Making it Your Own

Why am I so Tired?

What happens to you when you're experiencing brain injury fatigue?

- Mental symptoms:_____

  _____

  _____

- Physical symptoms:_____

  _____

  _____

- Emotional symptoms:_____

  _____

  _____

- Other symptoms:_____

  _____

  _____

What was your biggest challenge in the early days after your brain injury?

_____

_____

_____

How have you coped with that challenge?

_____

_____

_____

_____

Why Don't People Believe Me?

January 2000—Six Months after Brain Injury

Dear First-Year Survivor Carole,

Your primary care physician recently referred you to a neurologist, because you continue to struggle with the overwhelming fatigue, sound and light sensitivity, difficulty concentrating and emotions that are all over the place. You've tried to return to work multiple times, never managing more than 10 hours a week and even that took everything out of you.

The neurologist does a CAT scan and an EEG, which are both normal. He then tells you that you're fine and need to 'Get off your ass and get a job'. (That's a direct quote). This is devastating. You begin to believe that perhaps the symptoms aren't real and you're making them all up. Yet you know that you can't just make them disappear, as much as you want to. You feel alone and lost, unsure what to do or where to go for help.

As a long-term survivor, here's what I've learned that I'd like to share with you. *When your injury is 'invisible', there will be many people who will not believe you.* This may include family, friends and unfortunately even some of the medical professionals you look to for guidance. They may think that you're exaggerating your symptoms. They may tell you to just 'Get over it' and get on with life. Extreme statements like 'Get off your ass and get a job' or even more innocent sounding ones such as 'Aren't you better yet?' and 'I know someone who had an awful brain injury and is fine now' are heartbreakingly common.

They can add insult to injury, heaping emotional trauma on top of the brain trauma.

The unspoken message is that you could be better if you put your nose to the grindstone, pushed through it and made up your mind to heal. There's a lot of misinformation out there about brain injury and many people don't know what they're talking about. It's very important to not give up when you encounter ignorance. Keep searching until you can surround yourself with a team that's knowledgeable about brain injury. You need people who can offer you support, strategies and hope, not blame and judgment.

With Love from your Future Self,

Carole
Long-Term Survivor Carole

Making it Your Own

Why Don't People Believe Me?

Who are the people in your life who believe in you? Your list may include family members, friends, medical professionals, other professionals, community members and brain injury peers.

_____

_____

_____

_____

What kinds of support do you need from them to keep moving forward?

_____

_____

_____

_____

Why Do I Need Strategies?

April 2000—Nine Months after Brain Injury

Dear First-Year Survivor Carole,

After the disastrous appointment with the neurologist and several more months of struggling unsuccessfully to return to teaching and music, your primary care physician has sent you to a physiatrist, a doctor who specializes in physical medicine and rehabilitation. He recommends that you stop trying to go back to work for at least three months in order to attend an outpatient brain injury rehabilitation program.

You're very relieved that someone believes you and doesn't dismiss the symptoms. However, you're scared by the idea that your injury is serious enough to require rehabilitation. At this point, you don't even know what brain injury rehabilitation is. Three months seems like an eternity, but you're excited by the thought that this program will fix you. You believe you'll be back to normal by the end of the three months.

When rehab begins, you're surprised that there's a lot of focus on learning strategies to cope with your deficits. You're very resistant to this approach. You want a cure for your brain injury, not strategies. You're scared that if you use strategies to get things done, then your brain isn't healing. It feels like giving up, letting the injury win. Back to normal is your only measure of success and you won't consider anything less.

As a long-term survivor, here's what I've learned that I'd like to share with you. *You need to do what works for your brain <u>right now</u>, not what used to work or what you wish would work.* Success with strategies will feel much better than repeated failures without them. There are many people who can offer you strategies to cope with brain injury. These include not only rehab therapists, but also family, friends, other medical professionals and fellow brain injury survivors.

There is no magic pill that can cure brain injury. Healing is a long, slow process and often involves accepting a new normal, which is very challenging. You don't have to process that all at once. It will take time.

Strategies will enhance your healing, not hold it back. Failing over and over again gouges huge chunks out of your self-esteem and confidence. Strategies will let you experience success and help you realize what you can do. Your successes will build on one another and motivate you to continue to move forward.

Listen to the people in your life who are trying to help you—family, friends, rehab therapists, other medical professionals, fellow brain injury survivors—and embrace the use of strategies they suggest. When you start small, find success and build on it, you have no idea how far you'll be able to go!

With Love from your Future Self,

Carole
Long-Term Survivor Carole

Making it Your Own

Why Do I Need Strategies?

How do you feel about using strategies?

_____

_____

Are you resisting strategies or have you embraced them?

_____

What strategies are you using?

_____

_____

_____

_____

What successes have you had with strategies?

_____

_____

_____

Conclusion

In summary, here's what I wish I knew during that first year post-injury.

- Rest as much as your brain needs
- Realize that brain injury is misunderstood by many
- Recognize the importance of using strategies

It took me years and a lot of help to learn these valuable pieces of wisdom. The reality is that even though knowing them earlier would have made my journey less painful, no amount of wisdom can ever make brain injury easy.

The brain injury road is a long, dark and twisty one. As survivors, each of us must traverse that road for ourselves in our own way and at our own pace. But when we share the lessons we learn along the way, we can light parts of the path for one another. Since we can't go back in time and change our journey, what we can do is take in wisdom as we move forward and use our experiences to help others. I hope my experience has offered some light for my fellow brain injury travelers.

Making it Your Own

If I Knew Then What I Know Now

What have you learned about brain injury that you would share with another survivor who's earlier in his or her journey?

_____

_____

_____

Taking it Further

What's one thing you learned from reading this chapter?

_____

_____

_____

What action are you ready to take?

_____

_____

_____

CHAPTER 3

Word by Word:
The Journey toward Acceptance

As you start to walk out on the way, the way appears.

~Rumi

Accepting brain injury is a journey of coming to terms with a new normal. It's not a journey of neat, step-by-step phases. It's messy, with lots of starts and stops and circling back. The journey toward acceptance is more like a constantly curving spiral than a straightforward path.

The spiral has a long tradition of being used as a symbol for the journey of life and the change process. The spiral can also represent strength in adversity. This is seen in nature; for example, when trees are subjected to harsh conditions, they sometimes grow in a spiral pattern. This makes them less likely to break from strong winds or heavy snow; their wood is more flexible. Spiral growth makes them more resilient to the stressful environment.

What's true in nature can also be true for us as brain injury survivors. As we spiral through the acceptance process, it's possible to develop greater strength and resilience.

However, before the strength come many challenges. The spiral journey is a difficult one. While no two brain injury acceptance journeys will be the same, many of us experience similar emotions. My own journey was a spiral of inching forward and sliding backward. I twisted through many emotions, including shock, disbelief, denial, anger, despair, sadness, disappointment, worry, embarrassment, frustration, grief, and fear before reaching the calm peace of acceptance.

I have a record of my brain injury acceptance journey in the writing I did at the time. Writing has always been a way for me to collect my thoughts and work through my feelings. Before my injury, I'd gone more than a year without missing a single day writing in my journal.

After my brain injury, writing became a struggle. Most days, my brain injury symptoms made writing impossible. I'd go months without writing anything.

When I did manage to write, often I could produce only a few sentences or paragraphs before the mental fatigue took over, forcing me to stop. Sometimes I wrote in a notebook. More often, I wrote on small, loose scraps of paper. I forgot to date most of my writing. However, I did save all of it.

Even though the timing of my writings was spread out and their length was short, they still helped me process my experience. I didn't realize it at the time, but I was also creating a real-time record of my brain injury acceptance process.

My writings document the spiral journey. They're a window into the struggle to accept a new life as a brain injury survivor. They also show how strength and resilience can grow from that struggle.

I hope you'll see some of yourself and your own spiral journey in the excerpts from my writing on the next few pages. Since I can't put my writings in chronological order, I've divided them into four broad categories. These were stages I spiraled in and out of on my journey toward acceptance:

- Denial and Lack of Awareness
- Feeling Lost and Confused
- Sadness, Anger and Loss
- Growing toward Acceptance

The Spiral Journey

The most important thing I'd like you to take from my writings is hope. They show that where you are now in your journey is not where you'll stay forever. It is possible to grow and to change how you think about brain injury.

You'll see that although I've now accepted brain injury and created a new life, I started out just as lost, scared and confused as anyone else. None of us know how to cope with brain injury at first.

Even when you're lost, it's important to believe that you can be found. Wherever you are in your personal spiral, I hope these writings are inspiration; you can move toward acceptance.

Although the writings below are all grouped together and put in an order, they weren't written like that originally. Each italicized bullet point was written at a different time. As you read them, notice if there are statements that describe where you are right now in your own brain injury acceptance journey. You may want to mark the ones that most strongly relate to your experience.

Denial and Lack of Awareness

After my brain injury, all I could think about at first was total recovery and getting back to normal. Anything less than that was unacceptable and unthinkable. I thought that if I tried hard enough, I would recover fully.

- *I have to get better.*
- *I just have to push through this.*
- *All I see for the future is trying to get back to where I was.*

Feeling Lost and Confused

The longer my brain injury symptoms continued, the more lost and confused I felt. I didn't understand why I couldn't get better. My usual strategy of pushing my way through a challenge didn't work. Failures were beginning to accumulate, and my sense of self had started to crumble.

- *I want this all to be over, to go back to normal.*
- *Nothing seems easy anymore. Everything is a struggle, a challenge.*
- *I feel confused and uncertain of who I am anymore.*
- *It's like part of me has died.*

- *I feel like I'm falling apart. The glue that's holding me together is cracked. I don't know what to do, how to figure it all out. I can't stop crying. I can't deal with this anymore.*

Sadness, Anger and Loss

As it gradually became clear that my old life was gone forever, feelings of sadness, anger and loss increased. Sometimes it felt like I was drowning in painful emotions. I was much more aware of and frustrated by my limitations. A happy life seemed gone forever.

- *Everything I ever imagined my life would be is different. No career, no marriage, no kids, no music.*
- *When I think too much about the past, the loss is much more painful. The pain is needles sticking into me everywhere, each a reminder of what used to be, of what I thought my life would be.*
- *I do not accept this. I don't know if I can bear the idea that I have limitations.*
- *I have days when it's next to impossible to do anything. My brain just isn't consistent anymore.*
- *I hate the person I am now. I hate feeling weak and scared and tired and inconsistent and overwhelmed.*
- *I'm not strong enough for this. I want the old me back. I really miss her. I can't live like this. I am nothing, a hollowed out version of who I used to be.*

Growing toward Acceptance

For years, I spiraled between time spent grieving the losses and time spent getting to know the new me. Ever so slowly, my primary focus turned to the present and what I could do. That was the beginning of acceptance. I started to recognize my own strength and resilience.

- *My old way of doing things just doesn't work anymore.*
- *Perhaps I can trust that all this means something, that it has a higher purpose. I can trust that I'm on the right path, even when I feel lost.*
- *Life has different plans for me. The losses have opened new doors.*
- *The progress I continue to make isn't about regaining the old Carole. It's about creating the new Carole.*
- *Moving on doesn't mean the sadness and loss completely go away. They just become a smaller segment of my daily existence. I'm learning that victory doesn't come from not having those feelings, but rather from knowing how to deal with them.*
- *I am bent but not broken. My life is not ruined, just changed. It will only be ruined if I allow myself to look at it that way.*
- *I can't change what is. I can't will my brain to do what it's not able to do. I can savor my accomplishments, be content with where I am now and continue to work toward my goals.*
- *I feel so much happier. It's amazing—even though there are lots of things I can't do, I can still feel very happy about who I am right now.*

Recording the Journey

I'm very glad I have these writings to look back at. Ultimately, it didn't matter that I couldn't journal the way I did before my brain injury. It didn't matter that I couldn't write very much at a time or for very long. What matters is that I wrote. What matters is that I did what I could do. Having a record of my journey reminds me where I started and how far I've come.

There are many ways to record your brain injury journey. I wrote, because that's how I like to process my experience. Journal writing is just one of many options. Here are some other possibilities:

- Pictures
- Video Recordings
- Audio Recordings
- A Blog
- Art
- Poetry
- Posts on Social Media

If you choose to record your brain injury journey, there is no right or wrong way to track your experience. It's about whatever works best for you.

As brain injury survivors, each of us travels our own spiral path, twisting, turning, circling back and moving forward. Sometimes the journey can seem never-ending. It may not seem like it now, but every place on that spiral is part of the path toward accepting brain injury.

Making it Your Own

The Journey toward Acceptance

Which section best describes where you are right now in your brain injury acceptance journey?

- ☐ Denial and Lack of Awareness
- ☐ Feeling Lost and Confused
- ☐ Sadness, Anger and Loss
- ☐ Growing toward Acceptance

- ☐ Other_____

How would you choose to record your brain injury journey?

- ☐ Journal Writing
- ☐ Pictures
- ☐ Video Recordings
- ☐ Audio Recordings
- ☐ A Blog
- ☐ Art
- ☐ Poetry
- ☐ Posts on Social Media

- ☐ Other_____

Taking it Further

What's one thing you learned from reading this chapter?

_____

_____

_____

What action are you ready to take?

_____

_____

_____

A Reading Option

Some of you reading this book may be going through it in order, from beginning to end. That's a great choice; I designed the book to work in that way. If that's how you're reading this book, you may not need the information in this section.

Beginning to end is not your only choice of how to read this book. I also designed it to work for those of you who may want to read the chapters in your own order. Each chapter is independent of the others. That gives you a lot of flexibility in how you experience this book. If you're reading in your own order, here's an option to consider. On the next page, I've divided the book up using the sections described in this chapter—Denial and Lack of Awareness; Feeling Lost and Confused; Sadness, Anger and Loss; Growing toward Acceptance. Underneath each of those sections is a list of chapters that I think would be especially useful for someone at that stage to read. If this reading option is helpful to you, I'm glad. If it's not, keep reading the book in whatever way works for you on your brain injury acceptance journey.

CHAPTER 4

Facing Forward: Overcoming Denial

You never find yourself until you face the truth.

~Pearl Bailey

Denial is a big obstacle to overcome on the path to brain injury acceptance. Breaking through it may take several years. Denial occurs when a life event is so scary or painful that we're unable to acknowledge or admit the truth of it to ourselves. Denial can happen after the death of a loved one, a relationship ending, a job loss, an accident or a health crisis, like brain injury. Because reality is just too hard to process or too much to bear, it seems unreal, like it can't be happening.

Denial can be protective for a while. It provides the breathing space needed in order to move toward acceptance. However, eventually, denial will get in the way of moving forward. There comes a time to accept what is and to move forward with a new reality, even though it's painful, especially at first. Letting go of denial is the beginning of acceptance.

Recognizing Denial

There are two types of denial that brain injury survivors cope with in varying degrees: psychological denial and organic denial. With psychological denial, on some level you know what the truth is: brain injury has changed you forever. However, that truth is too much to bear right at first and too scary to fully admit to yourself.

With organic denial, the brain injury itself has made you unaware of your deficits. You believe you're just fine, but in truth your brain is lying to you. Organic denial is much more difficult to overcome. In general, more severe brain injuries result in worse cases of organic denial. Severe organic denial is outside both my experience and the scope of this book.

It took me about 5 years to stop denying my brain injury and its symptoms and to let go of returning to my old life. I think of denial like a gigantic boulder that blocks the path to acceptance. Here's what it was like when I was deep in denial, blocked by that boulder. As you read these bulleted statements, think about whether any of them ring true for you too.

- There was a frantic voice inside me that yelled over and over again, 'NO, NO, NO. This CAN'T be real.'
- Every morning, I hoped I would wake up 'normal' and the nightmare of the crushing mental fatigue, overwhelming sound and light sensitivity, difficulty managing everyday tasks, inability to make even simple decisions, memory challenges, slow thinking, and general confusion would just magically be over.
- I thought that if I just pushed harder and tried harder, I could make the brain injury go away.

- I felt embarrassed by my brain injury symptoms and tried to minimize and hide them from my family, friends and medical professionals.
- I wouldn't listen to suggestions from my family and friends.
- I often overestimated what I could do and was shocked and devastated when I failed.
- I refused to use strategies to get things done.
- I believed that the only way forward was to continue to push relentlessly to return to my old life as a teacher and amateur classical musician, even though I'd tried and failed many, many times to do that.

Awareness of the issue is the first step in overcoming denial. I wish I could tell you an easy way to take a sledgehammer to the boulder of denial. Unfortunately, there are no shortcuts in overcoming denial. It's a boulder that you can't skirt around, over or under. You have to work your way through it, at your own pace and in your own time. Overcoming denial is a process, one that can be particularly difficult, given the nature of brain injury. It definitely was for me. Be patient with yourself.

Making it Your Own

Recognizing Denial

Can you relate to any of these descriptions of denial?

- ☐ A voice inside yelling 'No, No, No. This can't be real.'
- ☐ Hoping to wake up 'normal' with no brain injury symptoms
- ☐ Believing that pushing more and trying harder will make your brain injury go away
- ☐ Feeling embarrassed by your brain injury symptoms
- ☐ Minimizing or hiding your brain injury symptoms from others
- ☐ Not listening to people who know you best
- ☐ Overestimating what you can do, then feeling shocked and devastated by failures
- ☐ Being unwilling to use strategies to get things done
- ☐ Pushing to return to the way life used to be

- ☐ Other_____

What's your reaction to the statements above about denial?

_____

_____

_____

_____

Overcoming Denial

If you've become aware that you have some denial going on, the next step is to start working through it. The metaphor I think about to explain the process of overcoming denial is planting seeds. Tremendous change can happen as a result of a slow process, like planting seeds. Once seeds take root and grow, they can eventually become strong enough to break through stone, to break through the boulder of denial.

Here are three seeds that over time grew to break down my boulder of denial:

- Learn about brain injury
- Connect with other survivors
- Reflect on failure.

Learn about Brain Injury

With any challenge, you have to understand what you're facing. Knowledge is a seed that can grow to break through denial. My knowledge journey began about eight months after my accident, when I bought my first book about brain injury.

I hadn't intended to purchase a brain injury book that day. I went into a bookstore looking for a gift for a friend and got overwhelmed, as often happened to me in stores then. I took refuge in an out-of-the-way corner and somehow ended up staring at a shelf of books on brain injury. Sometimes I think that the universe pushes us in the direction we need to grow.

With much trepidation, I purchased a book on mild traumatic brain injury that day. Due to my brain injury symptoms, I struggled to read that book; I had to go back and re-read sections many times. Despite this struggle, I saw myself and my symptoms in the pages of the book. That recognition was both terrifying and comforting for me. I wanted to run away from the words on the pages of that book and I wanted to learn more, both at the same time. Confronting denial is often a scary process at first, with lots of conflicting emotions.

The book was a good early denial busting tool, because I was learning about myself and my brain injury at a pace that I could handle. That's an important point. Overcoming denial has to happen at your pace. No one can force you to move faster. Trying to rush the process will only overwhelm you and set you back emotionally. Seeds grow in their own time.

The more I learned about brain injury, the greater my thirst for more knowledge became, and the more my boulder of denial cracked. I encourage you to learn as much as you can about brain injury. The better you understand brain injury, the better able you will be to move forward.

Making it Your Own

Learn about Brain Injury

What kinds of resources are you using to learn about brain injury?

☐ Books
☐ Websites
☐ Videos
☐ Magazines
☐ Conversations with medical professionals
☐ Brain injury support group
☐ Webinars
☐ Social media
☐ Other_____

What information about brain injury would be most helpful for you to know more about right now?

☐ Symptoms
☐ Treatments
☐ Coping strategies
☐ Survivor stories
☐ Other_____

What resources can you use to find that information?

_____

_____

Connect with Other Survivors

As much as family, friends and medical professionals support us, it's hard to understand the brain injury journey unless you've lived it. There's a special magic that happens when brain injury survivors talk to one another because we 'get it'. Connecting with peers, especially those who are further along the path, can give you a mirror into your own journey. Peers can plant seeds that grow toward overcoming denial.

It was a fellow brain injury survivor who planted the first seed that helped me overcome my denial about the need to use strategies. She was able to show me their importance in a way that no one else could. We met at an outpatient brain injury rehab program when I was about two years post-injury. We were both part of a strategies for living with brain injury group.

However, even at two years post-injury, I was still resisting the need for strategies to get things done, and I didn't get much out of the group. Denial was very strong in me. I wanted a brain injury cure, not strategies. I thought that if I used strategies, then I was letting the injury win and wasn't healing. I hadn't yet realized that success with strategies is a much better option than failing without them.

Once the strategies group ended, my new friend and I continued to get together on our own. We met once a month for lunch to talk about our progress, our struggles, fears, hopes and eventually even strategies. Because her injury was several years older than mine, I listened to her. I respected that she knew more than I did about living with brain injury. I wanted to reach the same level of acceptance she'd found. What she said about needing to use strategies reinforced what my therapists, as well as my family and friends, had been trying to tell me, the truth that I'd struggled to accept. Because peers share our journey, sometimes it's easier to hear hard truths from them.

Eventually, I joined a brain injury support group and met others like myself. As we swapped stories and shared our heartbreaks and triumphs, I saw myself in their experiences and felt less alone. Seeing more survivors using strategies and being successful opened me up further to using them and my boulder of denial cracked more.

Brain injury survivors who've trod the path from denial to acceptance can provide a unique form of support. Connecting with others who share the same journey can help you break through denial.

Making it Your Own

Connect with Other Survivors

What options do you have to connect with other brain injury survivors in your area?

- ☐ In-person peer mentoring
- ☐ Phone conversations
- ☐ Emails
- ☐ Brain injury support group
- ☐ Online brain injury support communities
- ☐ State Brain Injury Association or Alliance
- ☐ Hospital or Rehabilitation facilities

☐ Other_____

What would you most like to learn from other brain injury survivors? If you're having trouble answering this question, the Table of Contents, Appendix and Index may give you some ideas.

_____

_____

_____

_____

_____

Reflect on Failure

After brain injury, many of us are confronted by repeated failures as we relearn skills and try unsuccessfully to go back to the way life used to be. It's very discouraging to fail at tasks that used to be easy. When we can reflect on and learn from those failures instead of repeating them over and over again, we're on our way to acceptance.

For about five years after my injury, I believed that I was going to get my old life back. I thought I was going to recover and return to teaching and music. In my mind, I just had to try harder.

Trying harder was the way I'd always dealt with any difficulty. However, that mindset didn't work anymore. My denial was so strong I couldn't see, even with strategies, that the door to my old life was closed forever. To modify a famous quote variously attributed to Confucius, Benjamin Franklin and Albert Einstein, '<u>Denial</u> is doing the same thing over and over again and expecting different results'.

I tried over and over again to return to the old Carole. Denial can become a long-standing pattern that's hard to overcome on one's own. Sometimes it takes another person to break it.

In this case, it was my counselor. One day, after I told her about my most recent return-to-old-life failure, she asked me this question: 'Is it possible for you to accept that you're not going to make a full recovery?' Sometimes all it takes is one question asked at the right time to break through denial. I learned later that this was a question she'd asked me many times and in many forms. Patience and persistence are also required in overcoming denial.

As I sobbed hysterically in response to my counselor's question, the fact that my old life was over seared through me in a way it never had before. Suddenly, I was able to reflect on what all those failures meant. I wasn't failing because I wasn't trying hard enough. I was failing because what I was attempting was too much for me. It was too much for my brain.

I think I needed to fail a lot before I was ready to listen and accept that my old life was indeed over. There are times when denial is chipped away at slowly and other times when it's blasted away suddenly. This was a blasting day. I finally stopped trying to go back to my previous life and the old Carole. I changed my focus toward accepting and learning to appreciate my current life and the new Carole.

Within every failure are lessons. Until we begin to learn from failure, we just keep making the same mistakes over and over again, perpetuating denial. With reflection comes understanding, and with that understanding, acceptance can take root.

Making it Your Own

Reflect on Failure

What's your reaction to the question 'Is it possible for you to accept that brain injury has changed you?'

_____

_____

_____

Describe a task you've struggled with or failed at.

_____

_____

What went wrong?

_____

_____

_____

What strategies could you use if you attempt this task another time?

_____

_____

_____

What lessons can you learn from this failure?

_____

_____

_____

Conclusion

Without question, overcoming denial was the longest and most challenging part of my brain injury journey. Moving beyond denial was crucial in the acceptance process. In my first five years post-injury, every single person who was trying to help me played a role in helping me overcome denial. Family, friends, fellow survivors, doctors, physical, occupational and speech therapists, social workers, psychologists, and other medical professionals all helped me to learn about my brain injury, to connect with other survivors, to reflect on my failures, and eventually, to accept my injury.

So, whether you're a survivor, family member or professional reading this book, please know that what you're doing makes a difference, even if sometimes it doesn't seem like it. You are planting seeds.

Moving beyond denial doesn't remove all the challenges of living with brain injury. It does pave the way to being able to live life in full acceptance of those challenges. Then the path is clear to discover new ways to live a fulfilling life.

Making it Your Own

Overcoming Denial

Which overcoming denial strategy is most helpful to you right now?

- ☐ Learn about brain injury
- ☐ Connect with other survivors
- ☐ Reflect on failure

Taking it Further

What's one thing you learned from reading this chapter?

_____

_____

_____

What action are you ready to take?

_____

_____

_____

CHAPTER 5

Beyond Denial: Lost in the Middle

In the middle of the journey of our life, I came to myself within a dark wood where the straight way was lost.

~Dante Alighieri

It's a scary time as denial fades and reality sinks in. Once you become aware that brain injury has changed you forever, what's next? It might be clear that your old life is over, but the path forward is still very uncertain. So many questions remain unanswered. Who am I? What's going to happen to me? How do I live this new life? Will I ever be a happy, productive and fulfilled person again?

Loss of one's sense of self can be a big challenge during this time. One tool that helped me when I didn't know myself anymore was a temporary definition of my new self. I needed to answer the question 'Who am I now?'

I wrote a series of statements that I knew were true about me. They were words I could live by while I was discovering my new self and finding my path forward. It's my hope that this chapter will encourage you to create your own *Who am I Now?* statements.

Grieving the Loss of Self

As denial gradually ended for me, I became more and more painfully aware of how much I'd lost. The contrast between the old Carole and the new Carole was very stark. I spent a lot of time thinking about who I used to be. I'd always been proud of my quick intellect and ability to achieve. Brain injury damaged those qualities I'd defined myself by, leaving me feeling lost and worthless.

I hated all the ways I'd changed and deeply mourned my loss of self. I doubted whether I was strong enough to cope with all of it. I was learning strategies, but I still worried a lot about what was going to happen to me in the future.

During this time, a friend recommended that I read the book *Transitions* by William Bridges. Even though I was still struggling with reading due to my brain injury, I gave it a try. I'm very glad I did, because *Transitions* was pivotal for me.

Even though all I could manage was slowly skimming the book's contents, I learned enough to get me thinking. That thinking led to a big *Eureka* moment and a strategy to help me cope with my loss of self. I didn't have to read every word in the book to get something out of it. Sometimes being good enough at a task is all that's needed to move forward.

A Strategy for Lost in the Middle

In *Transitions*, Bridges explains that between the ending of an old way of life and the beginning of a new way is a challenging middle period filled with confusion, distress and uncertainty. He called it the neutral zone. That resonated with how I felt back then. It was as if I existed in a no-man's land. My pre-brain injury life had ended, but I didn't yet know how to live successfully as a brain injury survivor. One of Bridges' recommendations for getting through the neutral zone was to 'arrange temporary structures'.

So what does 'arrange temporary structures' mean? Here's an analogy to help explain it. Imagine an earthquake has destroyed your house. It's gone and you need to build a new one, which is going to take a lot of time. Meanwhile, you need somewhere safe to live, a temporary structure. That could be staying with family or friends, renting an apartment or staying in a hotel. The temporary structure is a strategy to bridge the divide between the end of the old and the start of the new.

Brain injury is like a personal earthquake. It leaves our lives in shambles and shakes us right down to the core of our being. It cracks the foundation of who we are, our sense of self. It takes a great deal of time, often years, to build something new. A temporary structure can help as we build our new sense of self. Here's how I applied the concept of temporary structures to my life.

After skimming the *Transitions* book many times, I wrote about what I'd learned. This was a helpful strategy for me to process and remember information. At first, I thought about temporary structures only in terms of how I was structuring my time. Back then, my occupational therapist was helping me create a weekly schedule that worked for me as a brain injury survivor. I was slowly learning how to balance medical appointments, time with family and friends, household chores and doable, fun activities with my absolute need for lots and lots of brain rest. That schedule helped me during the neutral zone and is one example of a temporary structure.

One day, seemingly out of the blue, I had another idea for how to use the concept of temporary structures. Now I recognize that all the thinking and writing I'd been doing about temporary structures had primed my idea pump. I remembered that a few months previously, I'd written a series of statements. They were beliefs that the old Carole had lived her life by. Here they are:

- *I always have high expectations of myself; perfection is my standard.*
- *Be busy all the time.*
- *Push harder when faced with adversity; I'm weak if I don't push.*
- *My achievements are what make me worthwhile as a person.*
- *I am dependable.*

In a sudden moment of insight, I realized that since brain injury had made me a new person, I could write new statements. I didn't have to continue trying to live according to my old way of thinking. I'd begun to realize that it was a rather harsh and unforgiving way to live anyway.

A Temporary Sense of Self

I wrote new statements that described what I knew about myself right then, as I was. They reflected what I had learned in my brain injury journey so far and what I was currently working toward becoming.

Since I was working on being less harsh with my new self, I tried to make the statements non-judgmental. I was trying to be more positive about my situation, so I avoided negative language. The statements represented the work in progress that I was. They were my temporary structure, my temporary sense of self, my *Who am I Now?* statements. Here's what I wrote:

- *I am learning new things about myself.*
- *I honor my mental fatigue and structure my activities accordingly.*
- *I forgive myself when I cannot meet my own expectations.*
- *I find what brings me joy and meaning.*
- *I am still a worthwhile person.*
- *Simple is good.*
- *Ultimately, this can all be viewed as a journey of self-discovery.*
- *Anytime can be nap time, and that's ok.*
- *I celebrate my successes, no matter how small.*
- *I focus on the present. The past is over and the future will take care of itself.*
- *I consistently do what is best for my health.*

Benefits of *Who am I Now?* Statements

These *Who am I Now?* statements filled the gap between my old self that was destroyed by brain injury and my new self that would emerge as I reached full acceptance. They provided tangible proof that I was on the right path and gradually working my way through the neutral zone. Every time I read them, I felt hope, strength and peace. They helped anchor me in the present when my thoughts drifted to either mourning the past or worrying about the future.

I also framed and hung my *Who am I Now?* statements on my wall. That act itself was also a temporary structure. At the time, the walls of my house were mostly bare, because I'd taken down all the pictures that reminded me of who I used to be. Seeing my *Who Am I Now?* statements on the wall, as well as recent poems I'd written and crafts I'd made, reminded me that I was building a new life and a new self.

Guidelines for *Who am I Now?* Statements

Would you like to write your own *Who Am I Now?* statements? If you do, here are a few guidelines:

- *Use positive or emotionally neutral language.* A sense of self built on negative statements will not help you move forward out of the neutral zone. Negativity will trap you there. If you have trouble framing your thoughts positively, ask a family member, friend or medical professional for help.
- *Write the statements in the present tense.* This will help you stay grounded in the present.
- *Display your Who am I Now? statements where you can see them every day.* Read them aloud a lot. The repetition will help the words become part of you.

Rebuilding one's sense of self is a necessary step in the journey toward acceptance after brain injury. *Who am I Now?* statements are a tool that can help with that process.

Making it Your Own

Beyond Denial

Think about your life before brain injury. How would you describe how you thought about yourself? What did the old you believe? You can look at my list on page 50 if you need ideas to begin.

_____

_____

_____

_____

What is positive and true about the person you are right now?

_____

_____

_____

Write your own *Who am I Now?* statements. Remember to use positive or emotionally neutral words. You can use my list on page 51 as a reference point if needed.

_____

_____

_____

_____

_____

_____

How can you remind yourself to read your *Who am I Now?* statements regularly?

_____

_____

Taking it Further

What's one thing you learned from reading this chapter?

_____

_____

_____

What action are you ready to take?

_____

_____

_____

CHAPTER 6

Resolutions for Brain Injury Survivors

Always bear in mind that your own resolution to succeed is more important than any other.

~Abraham Lincoln

After brain injury, it's common to look at the past and grieve who we used to be. There's so much loss to process; it may seem impossible to face a future with a brain that doesn't work the same anymore. There are mindsets that can support us while we work on gradually accepting our new selves.

When you resolve to incorporate these ways of thinking into your life, you can begin to transition from looking backward at the past to facing forward toward the future. You can begin to move from surviving to thriving after brain injury.

Resolutions are something most of us associate with January 1st. Some scholars say that the month of January was named for the ancient Roman god Janus. Janus had two faces looking in opposite directions. One stared backward toward the past, while the other gazed forward toward the future. Because Janus simultaneously looked at the past and future, he symbolized beginnings and endings and transition spaces like doorways and bridges. Janus is the perfect symbol for the New Year, when many people take the time to reflect on their lives over the previous twelve months and to plan ahead for the next twelve.

Janus can also be a symbol for the brain injury acceptance process. Whatever the date of your brain injury, that day becomes a metaphorical January 1st. It's the date that sharply divides your life into two halves. Our language reflects that divide. We talk about our old self vs. our new self and our old life vs. our new life. Every moment in life is categorized as happening either before the brain injury or after the brain injury.

Acceptance can be defined as being like Janus and looking at both the past and the future. When we've accepted brain injury, we're able to acknowledge the past without getting overwhelmed by emotion. At the same time, we're able to face the future and live within a new normal.

I spent many years after my brain injury looking backward at the life and the self I lost. I mourned deeply who I'd been and the promise that seemed to be gone. A future living with brain injury deficits seemed much too scary and depressing to even consider. It took me about eight years to work through that heavy grief and to transition to facing forward into acceptance of my new life as a brain injury survivor.

If you're someone who feels stuck right now looking back at the past, you may be wondering something like this: 'But how can I transition from looking backward to looking forward?' One thing I learned in my own brain injury journey was that how I thought about my experience mattered. I couldn't control the brain injury, but I did have some control over how I thought about it. There were some mindsets that kept me trapped in all the loss and others that facilitated my movement forward. Our thoughts can have great power.

Below are five mindsets that helped me in my journey to acceptance. I hope they're helpful in yours too. I've worded these mindsets as resolutions, because that turns them into items for action. Acceptance is an action-oriented process. It's with resolve that we can turn toward the future.

These resolutions won't be accomplished overnight or even all at once. They require time, patience and persistence. As you read the resolutions, note which one or ones stand out for you. That will give you clues where you're ready to grow and begin to face forward.

I Resolve to Recognize and Celebrate my Progress

No matter how slow and uneven the progress happens or how small and inconsequential the gains may seem, I will savor every step forward. My successes will build on one another.

I Resolve to Stop Comparing

It's not fair to compare my new self to who I used to be or to compare my brain injury to others' brain injuries. Both types of comparison only set me up for extra grief and feeling inferior. Instead, I'll use the day of my brain injury as my starting point. It will be my personal

New Year's and I'll measure my progress from there. My journey is my own and will not match anyone else's.

I Resolve to be Gentle with Myself when I Fail

I'm doing my best. Every failure gives me an opportunity to learn and grow.

I Resolve to Find an Activity that my Current Self is Good at and Can Enjoy

The more I focus on what I <u>can</u> do, the better I'll feel about myself.

I Resolve to Trust that my Life can Still be Good

Where I am right now in my journey isn't where I'll always be. I'll continue to grow, to change and to learn. My life may never be the same again, but it doesn't have to be ruined.

When I was working on incorporating these resolutions into my life, I had copies of them strategically placed in various locations around my house. That way I had to read them multiple times a day. This helped them gradually seep into my way of thinking. I even framed some of them and hung them on my wall.

The resolutions were also the topic of many conversations with my family, friends, brain injury support group and various medical professionals. They gently encouraged me when my thoughts were stuck and all I could see was everything I'd lost to brain injury.

Resolutions like these can help us move from looking backward at the past to looking forward to the future. I encourage you to think about ways to incorporate them into your own life.

Making it Your Own

Resolutions

Which Janus face best represents where you are right now—the face looking backward or the face looking forward?

_____

_____

Which resolution challenges you the most?

- ☐ I resolve to recognize and celebrate my progress
- ☐ I resolve to stop comparing
- ☐ I resolve to be gentle with myself when I fail
- ☐ I resolve to find an activity that my current self is good at and can enjoy
- ☐ I resolve to trust that my life can still be good

Which resolution(s) are you ready to move forward with?

- ☐ I resolve to recognize and celebrate my progress
- ☐ I resolve to stop comparing
- ☐ I resolve to be gentle with myself when I fail
- ☐ I resolve to find an activity that my current self is good at and can enjoy
- ☐ I resolve to trust that my life can still be good

How could you incorporate that resolution into your life?

_____

_____

_____

Write your own resolution that can help you move forward.

I Resolve to: _____

_____

_____

Taking it Further

What's one thing you learned from reading this chapter?

_____

_____

_____

What action are you ready to take?

_____

_____

_____

CHAPTER 7

Word Power: Change your Words, Change your Brain

If you can change your mind, you can change your life.

~William James

Brain injury has ruined my life. I'm so stupid. All I do is make mistakes. I'm useless. I can't do anything anymore.

Do any of those statements sound familiar? Have you said words like these to yourself? They're all words that I've thought and said about myself before. As you read those statements, how do you feel? I can feel stress building in my system, a knot in my stomach and sadness taking over me. I feel paralyzed, unable to act. I want to hide in shame. These are not words that heal. These are not words that lead toward brain injury acceptance.

How can we counteract the harsh statements that so many of us say to ourselves? One strategy is to trade the negative language for positive language. Let's experiment and start this chapter over with some different words. Read or say each one slowly and allow it to roll over you.

Peace   patience   trust   kindness   joy   learning   forgiveness

How do you feel after reading those words? I feel the stress of the other sentences melting away. I feel lighter inside, calmer and more optimistic.

Words are powerful tools in the journey toward brain injury acceptance. The words you use matter a lot. They can hold you back or they can move you forward. Scientific research has demonstrated that negative words, repeated over and over, can disrupt brain chemistry. The brain interprets negative self-talk as an actual, real-life threat. Words are as real as actions to our brains.

When your brain feels threatened, the defenses of fight, flight or freeze can get activated. You may want to lash out, run away or stop in your tracks. Over time, the brain chemicals released by negative self-talk can damage the brain's memory and emotion centers. Yes, words can cause brain damage! As brain injury survivors, we've all got enough damage to deal with.

Even when we want to turn off the negative words, it's a task that may be easier said than done. Negative self-talk can be a hard habit to break, especially if it's been a long-standing one. That certainly was true for me. Even before my brain injury, I was really hard on myself. As a Type A high achiever, my standard was perfection. I criticized myself mercilessly whenever I didn't live up to that ideal. My self-worth was based on how much I could do and how well and how fast I could do it.

After my brain injury, failure became a regular occurrence as I tried unsuccessfully to return to my old life. Every time I failed, my thoughts grew darker. My negative self-talk often took over when I struggled with once-easy tasks or when brain injury fatigue incapacitated me. I called myself stupid, lazy and worthless.

One of the unexpected gifts of my brain injury has been the opportunity to learn to be kinder to myself. With time, practice and help, I've mostly tamed my negative self-talk. Looking back through my experience, I've identified three strategies that helped me. They are:

- Use inspirational words
- Repeat positive affirmations
- Talk back to negative language

I can't take credit for inventing any of these strategies. I learned them from my counselor. When negative self-talk is ingrained, like it was for me, professional help can be useful.

Use Inspirational Words

Since my brain injury, three words that inspire me are trust, patience and joy. They're inscribed on three small stones that I keep on my desk. For many years, I brought them with me whenever I attempted something new or challenging. Yes, my purse had rocks in it! Whenever my negative thinking started to overwhelm me, I looked at those words—trust, patience, joy. They reminded me to trust the process, be patient with myself and focus on what brings me joy.

Think about words that bring you feelings of peace, optimism and hopefulness. These can be tools to help combat negative self-talk. It's about making a conscious decision to focus on words that inspire you instead of words that make you feel worse.

The inspirational words technique can also be adapted. Words aren't the only way to tame negative language. Think about what moves you. What puts you in a positive frame of mind? Instead of words, you could use a meaningful picture to look at, an inspirational piece of music to listen to or a favorite object to hold. When negative self-talk starts to take over your mind, it's important to have your own strategy to break the cycle.

Making it Your Own

Use Inspirational Words

Below is a list of positive words. Which three words mean the most to you?

- ☐ Acceptance
- ☐ Balance
- ☐ Confidence
- ☐ Forgiveness
- ☐ Honesty
- ☐ Independence
- ☐ Kindness
- ☐ Love
- ☐ Pride
- ☐ Strength
- ☐ Truth
- ☐ Appreciation
- ☐ Beauty
- ☐ Contentment
- ☐ Fun
- ☐ Hope
- ☐ Insight
- ☐ Laughter
- ☐ Meaning
- ☐ Respect
- ☐ Transformation
- ☐ Whole
- ☐ Awakening
- ☐ Calmness
- ☐ Courage
- ☐ Gratitude
- ☐ Humor
- ☐ Joy
- ☐ Learning
- ☐ Patience
- ☐ Safety
- ☐ Trust
- ☐ Wisdom

If you can't find three words that inspire you, add your own positive words.

_____

_____

How could you keep these three words visible throughout your day?

_____

_____

What other strategies could you use to interrupt negative self-talk?

☐ This picture to look at:_____

☐ This music to listen to:_____

☐ This object to hold:_____

Repeat Positive Affirmations

According to psychological research, it takes three to five positives to counteract the effect of one negative. Affirmations are short, positive statements you can use to replace negative self-talk.

Below are some of the affirmations that I've used. With time and repetition, these statements helped override my voice inside that said that I wasn't trying hard enough, that I was a failure and that my life was over.

- *I'm doing the best I can*
- *I'm ok just as I am right now*
- *I'm learning how to cope with brain injury*
- *It's ok if I don't handle things perfectly*
- *I focus on finding the small joys in the present*
- *I believe that something good can come from brain injury*
- *I'm slowly finding my way*

The most effective affirmations are ones that you can believe. They should ring true for you. Otherwise, every time you say the affirmation, there will probably be a part of you scornfully saying 'Yeah, right'. That won't help eliminate negative self-talk; it will strengthen it.

The power of an affirmation is in its repetition. The more times you repeat an affirmation, the stronger it becomes and the more it can sink into your consciousness. I wrote my affirmations on pieces of paper that I taped to my computer screen and to my refrigerator, so I could see and say them regularly. Here are some additional options to keep your affirmations visible:

- Write an affirmation on a mirror and say it as you look at your reflection. (Be sure to use an erasable marker!)
- Post affirmations on your door and read them every time you leave the house
- Make an affirmation into a screen saver on your computer or lock screen on your phone
- Use an affirmation app

Affirmations can be ones you write yourself. They can also be quotes from others that speak to you. For example, whenever I had a bad brain day, I channeled my inner Scarlett O'Hara from *Gone with the Wind*. In my best Maine-born version of a southern accent, I reminded myself that 'Tomorrow is another day!'

Making it Your Own

Repeat Positive Affirmations

What's one common negative statement you say to yourself?

- ☐ Brain injury has ruined my life.
- ☐ I'm so stupid.
- ☐ All I do is make mistakes.
- ☐ I'm useless.
- ☐ I can't do anything anymore.

- ☐ Other_____

Choose or write 3-5 affirmations you can use to counteract that negative self-talk. They should be statements you can believe.

- ☐ I'm doing the best I can
- ☐ I'm ok just as I am right now
- ☐ I'm learning how to cope with brain injury
- ☐ It's ok if I don't handle things perfectly
- ☐ I focus on finding the small joys in the present
- ☐ I believe that something good can come from brain injury
- ☐ I'm slowly finding my way

- ☐ Other_____

- ☐ Other_____

- ☐ Other_____

How can you repeat your affirmations regularly?

- ☐ Tape affirmations to the refrigerator and read them before opening the door
- ☐ Write an affirmation on a mirror (using erasable marker) and say it while looking at your reflection.
- ☐ Post affirmations on the door and read them before leaving the house
- ☐ Tape affirmations in front of your computer screen and read them before turning on the computer
- ☐ Make an affirmation into a computer screen saver or phone lock screen
- ☐ Use an affirmation app

- ☐ Other idea_____

- ☐ Other idea_____

Talk Back to Negative Language

Have you noticed that when dark thoughts enter your head, they often get stuck there? Once the cycle of negative self-talk starts, it can be hard to break free. One reason for that is called the negativity bias. As a species, our brains developed to pay more attention to the negative than the positive, a trait that helped ensure survival. This bias means it's all too easy for negative self-talk to dominate our lives.

Just because our brains are wired to pay more attention to the negative, it doesn't mean we have to live there. It also doesn't mean those negative thoughts are true. It's possible to challenge our thoughts and break the cycle of negative self-talk.

My own negative self-talk often jumped to the worst case scenario. If I failed at one task, it meant I was doomed to fail at everything. If I needed help from my family and friends, it meant I was a burden to them. My counselor helped me learn how to talk back to my negative thinking by asking me this series of questions:

- *What evidence is there that your negative thought is true?*
- *What evidence is there that your negative thought is not true?*
- *What's the worst thing that that could happen?*
- *What's the best thing that could happen?*
- *What's a more balanced way to look at the situation?*
- *What advice would you give a friend who's going through the same situation?*

Working through these questions took some of the power out of my negative self-talk. The process of asking and answering them helped me feel more hopeful about my situation. The more I practiced using them, the better I got at turning off my negative thoughts and replacing them with more positive ones.

Part of accepting brain injury is accepting ourselves. When the way we talk about ourselves is harsh and demeaning, acceptance stays out of reach. Using positive words, repeating affirmations and talking back to negative language are strategies that can tame negative self-talk. When we change our words, we change our brains, paving the way forward toward acceptance.

Making it Your Own

Talk Back to Negative Language

The questions below are challenging. It's not easy to talk back to negative language. You may want to consider working through this section with another person, such as a family member, friend or professional.

What negative thought would you like to talk back to?

_____

_____

What evidence is there that your negative thought is true?

_____

_____

What evidence is there that your negative thought is not true?

_____

_____

What's the worst thing that could happen?

_____

_____

What's the best thing that could happen?

_____

_____

What's a more balanced way to look at the situation?

_____

_____

What advice would you give a friend who's going through the same situation?

_____

_____

Taking it Further

What's one thing you learned from reading this chapter?

_____

_____

_____

What action are you ready to take?

_____

_____

_____

CHAPTER 8

Crafting a New Life

When one door of happiness closes, another opens; but often we look so long at the closed door that we do not see the one which has been opened before us.

~Helen Keller

When your life has been shattered by brain injury and the door to your old life has not just closed, but slammed shut, how do you find a new door of happiness and acceptance? Where do you look? How do you begin? Below is a list of actions that gradually helped me in my journey from banging against the closed door of my old life to walking through the open door of my new life. I hope they can help you too.

- Get to know your new self
- Listen for the wisdom of the little voice inside
- Take action
- Start small, find success and build on it
- Find ways to give to others
- Take risks: Feel the fear and move forward anyway
- Make something: Create meaning out of suffering

Get to Know Your New Self

Brain injury changes who you are and what you know about yourself. Many of us feel like different people, with new and unfamiliar limitations, reactions, thoughts, feelings, fears, likes and dislikes. We're strangers to ourselves. The last thing many of us want to do is get to know the new person we've become. I know I hated the new Carole for a long time after my injury. I wanted to distance myself from her. I didn't think there could be anything to like about her.

However, the more I tried to ignore the new Carole, the more stuck I stayed in denial, in loss and in grief over what might have been. I had no chance of finding my new door of happiness and acceptance until I turned away from the old one.

A crucial step in turning away from that old door was getting to know the new me. I had to develop self-knowledge. The importance of self-knowledge has been recognized for millennia, as evidenced by this wisdom from the ancient Greek philosopher Socrates: 'Know thyself'.

In an instant, brain injury changes the self-knowledge you've accumulated over your entire life. Getting to know your new self is kind of like growing up all over again. When you grew up the first time, others helped you figure out who you were. That same process can work again after brain injury.

My family and friends helped me gain a lot of self-knowledge. They suggested new activities that brought joy to my life. They reassured me that the new Carole was still good at many things. They focused my attention on the times when I felt proud of myself. They helped me gain greater awareness of my challenges and struggles.

It was hard for me to accept help from those who had known me as a competent, independent adult in my pre-brain injury life. I didn't like feeling dependent on them. Often I felt like a confused child. However, eventually I learned that dependence on others was a necessary part of my path to self-knowledge and greater independence.

You can get to know your new self by listening to observations from your team—trusted medical professionals, family, friends, other brain injury survivors and members of the community. Especially early on, they often see what you're not able to recognize. They can help you begin to understand who you are now, find your strengths and work on your weaknesses.

Nothing about brain injury is quick and easy. Getting to know and even like your new self is a process, one that takes time. It means focusing on the present, on what is. That's how you begin to find the door to your new life.

Making it Your Own

Get to Know your New Self

Who are the members of your team who could help you get to know your new self? Your team may include family members, friends, other brain injury survivors, community members, medical and other types of professionals.

_____

_____

_____

_____

_____

What brings joy into your life right now?

_____

_____

_____

_____

What are you good at now?

_____

_____

_____

_____

What do you struggle with?

_____

_____

_____

_____

When do you feel pride?

_____

_____

_____

_____

Listen for the Wisdom of the Little Voice Inside

When you're focused on knowing yourself in the present, the door to a new life has begun to crack open. I believe all of us have a little voice, an inner wisdom that can offer guidance about how to further open that door. It's a quiet voice, one that can't be heard when you're living in the past and trying desperately to get back to the way life used to be.

My little voice inside didn't come out until I stopped trying to go back to teaching and music. I had to stop trying to be the old Carole. My inner wisdom came out when I focused on the present and the new Carole.

As I focused on my present, I observed within me a new desire to make things. I wanted to use my hands to create, which was something I'd never done before. My little voice inside was whispering 'make something'.

This was surprising to me, because I'd never been interested in hands-on activities pre-injury. My inner voice was pointing me in a new direction. Sometimes we just have to trust the wisdom of our inner voice and see where it leads us.

How do you access the little voice inside? It doesn't tend to come out on command. Hearing it requires patience.

My little voice inside seems to come out when I'm alone and doing a quiet but engaging activity. Activities that work well are ones that keep me focused, but don't take up all of my cognitive energy. Many of them also have a rhythmic quality to them. Some of my best insights have come to me while meditating, journal writing, taking a walk, weeding the garden, washing the dishes or even just taking a shower.

The little voice inside is like a compass, pointing you in the direction of your new life. When you can hear and act on its wise counsel, you are on your way.

Making it Your Own

Listen for the Wisdom of the Little Voice Inside

What's a quiet, present-focused activity you can do to access your little voice inside?

☐ Meditate
☐ Write in a journal
☐ Take a walk
☐ Weed the garden
☐ Wash the dishes
☐ Take a shower

☐ Other _____

If you can hear your little voice inside, what direction does it point you in?

_____

_____

_____

_____

Take Action

It isn't enough just to observe the little voice inside. You have to act on it. Observation without action won't get you anywhere. Actions don't have to be big and grand to have a major impact. Even the smallest of actions can open new doors.

Acting on my quiet voice inside that said 'make something' was a turning point for me. It was the first time that I turned away from beating loudly and unsuccessfully at the closed door of my old life and toward opening the new one.

At first, I didn't know what action to take in response to my inner voice's 'make something' guidance. I had no idea what to make. I went to the craft store once, got overwhelmed and left with nothing.

Feeling discouraged, I talked to a friend, who suggested I try paint-by-number. Taking action often requires some assistance. My second trip to the craft store was successful. I went right to the paint-by-number section and picked out a mosaic picture of a sun. I liked it because the pattern was pretty and bright and seemed doable.

When taking action, small and simple is the best way to start. With brain injury, that's often the only way we can start. Because of my difficulties with fatigue, concentration and attention, I could only work at my paint-by-number for fifteen minutes at a time and then had to take a nap. Despite the challenge, I loved making something. My inner voice had pointed me in a good direction.

Taking action made me feel better about myself. I looked forward every day to working on the paint-by-number. I could see how it was helping my attention and concentration, as I was able to work at it for longer times. I started to feel like I was once again moving forward, at my own pace. Taking action is good for self-esteem and self-confidence.

Actions build on one another. Successfully finishing that paint-by-number spurred me on to try other crafts, such as jewelry making, cross-stitching and photography. I don't think it matters where you start or what you start with, just that you do. Once you take one action, more can follow as you gain momentum.

Making it Your Own

Take Action

What's one small action you can take?

_____

_____

_____

_____

What help do you need to get started?

_____

_____

_____

_____

Start Small, Find Success and Build on It

Whatever action you choose, it's important to start where you can succeed. Finding that success often means you have to break down tasks into very small pieces. You may need help from your team to break down tasks. I know I did. How small should tasks be? As small as they need to be for you to experience success.

I can't stress enough how important success is. Brain injury tends to rob us of feelings of success. Many of us fail over and over at previously simple tasks. Those repeated failures can damage self-confidence and self-esteem.

My own self-confidence and self-esteem were both at rock bottom after my brain injury. When I began having success creating and completing crafts, it was like a shot of adrenalin for my psyche. The more success I experienced, the more motivated I became to continue building my new life and to continue moving forward, one tiny step at a time.

Actions you can succeed at will propel you forward. When you find something you can do successfully, no matter how small it is, that's where you build from.

Making it Your Own

Start Small, Find Success and Build on It

Write down an action you would like to take.

_____

What are the small steps needed to accomplish this action?

_____

_____

_____

What difficulties could you face while taking this action?

_____

_____

_____

What strategies would help you be successful?

_____

_____

_____

Who can you ask for help if you need it?

_____

_____

Write down a task you've failed at.

_____

How could you turn that task into a success?

- ☐ Break it down into smaller pieces?
- ☐ Use a different strategy?
- ☐ Ask for help?
- ☐ Decide it's too big to attempt right now?

- ☐ Other idea_____

What's an activity you're successful at right now?

_____

_____

_____

Find Ways to Give to Others

Giving to others is a win-win activity, with both the receiver and the giver benefiting. Besides the general feeling of satisfaction that comes from giving, there are also health benefits. These can include lower stress levels, lower blood pressure, decreased depression, increased self-esteem, greater happiness, and a longer life.

Brain injury can make finding ways to give to others challenging. Often we have to find new ways to give, since our old ways may not work anymore.

Ways to give don't have to be big and grand. Brain injury taught me just how powerful small gestures can be. Things like a card, a phone call, an e-mail, a hug, a plate of muffins or a bouquet of flowers can mean the world to someone who's going through a rough time. There are many simple ways to give to others and show how much you care.

Crafts helped me find my new way to give. I began giving items I made to family and friends as gifts. It was so exciting to see how pleased they were to receive something that I created for them. Making gifts was a rewarding way to spend my time.

Even though I still needed a lot of help from my family and friends, I began to realize that I could give to them too. I didn't always have to be on the receiving end of help. Through giving, I began to feel less like a professional patient and bottomless pit of need. I gradually began to like myself again.

Crafts opened another door for me. At the rehab hospital where I received outpatient treatment, I taught other brain injury survivors how to make jewelry. This led me back to teaching, another way to give.

Finding ways to give made me feel useful again and more a part of the world. The more I gave, the better I felt about myself. It became easier to accept my new life and to see that some good was coming from it. Finding ways to give to others can open the door to acceptance and happiness.

Making it Your Own

Find Ways to Give to Others

How do you currently give to others?

_____

_____

_____

What's a new way you could try to give to others?

- ☐ Send a card
- ☐ Make a phone call
- ☐ Send an e-mail
- ☐ Give a hug
- ☐ Send flowers
- ☐ Bake something
- ☐ Make something

- ☐ Other idea_____

When you give to others, what emotions do you experience?

_____

_____

_____

Take Risks: Feel the Fear and Move Forward Anyway

When cognition doesn't work right due to brain injury, the world can seem dangerous. It's easy to become isolated. Experiencing failure after failure can make us extra cautious and scared to try anything new.

Moving forward into a new life means taking some risks. I don't mean negative risks that are impulsive and can lead to dangerous situations. Instead, I mean positive risks that are calculated and can lead to growth, increased confidence and new opportunities.

My most important calculated risk came four years after my brain injury. I was asked to participate in a workshop on creativity at my state brain injury conference. This meant displaying my crafts and talking about how they'd helped me as a brain injury survivor. It was my first opportunity to speak publicly about my brain injury.

Sharing my story in front of others felt risky, because at that time I was still very embarrassed by my brain injury symptoms. I was afraid I would get overwhelmed and wouldn't be able to talk. As a former teacher and musician, I knew how to deal with performance jitters, but brain injury had erased all my confidence. My legs shook from nerves the entire time I spoke, but I did it.

Pushing my boundaries at that conference had many benefits. My self-esteem and self-confidence increased. I experienced the power of using my story to help others. I began to feel like there could be some value and purpose in all that I'd been through.

When I spoke at that conference, it felt like I was coming 'home', and for the first time since my accident, my way forward was clear. I knew that speaking about brain injury was what I wanted to do.

That calculated risk was the beginning of more opportunities. Doors opened that I never could have foreseen. Taking risks can push us in new directions we couldn't have imagined. Over the years, I've gone from being part of panel discussions, to giving short talks, organizing workshops, delivering keynote speeches and writing this book.

In 2010, my mentor Bev Bryant and I founded the survivor group Brain Injury Voices (BrainInjuryVoices.org). As a group, we volunteer approximately 2500 hours each year as brain injury educators, advocates and peer mentors. I still cannot hold a job, but I do have a career, one that started with taking a risk—by being afraid but choosing to move forward anyway.

Here are some examples of calculated risks:

- Trying a different coping strategy
- Seeing a new medical provider
- Getting out of the house
- Socializing with others
- Doing something new
- Sharing your story
- Attending a brain injury support group
- Going to a brain injury conference

Taking calculated risks can push your boundaries in a positive direction. When you begin to stretch yourself, life becomes richer.

Making it Your Own

Take Risks: Feel the Fear and Move Forward Anyway

What's an activity you'd like to do, but feel apprehensive about trying? Below are some possibilities to get your thinking started.

☐ Try a different coping strategy
☐ See a new medical provider
☐ Get out of the house
☐ Socialize with others
☐ Do something new
☐ Share your story
☐ Attend a brain injury support group
☐ Go to a brain injury conference

☐ Other _____

What's a small risk you can take to begin moving forward with that activity?

_____

_____

_____

Make Something: Create Meaning out of Suffering

None of us asked for a brain injury. None of us chose the physical, mental and emotional devastation that it causes. None of us wanted to have our lives uprooted. So many choices are taken from us with brain injury. However, one thing we can choose is to turn all that suffering into something meaningful. As the German philosopher Friedrich Nietzsche said, 'To live is to suffer; to survive is to find some meaning in the suffering'.

My journey forward began when I listened to the little voice inside me that whispered 'make something'. I didn't recognize it then, but the words 'make something' are about so much more than just doing something with my hands. They also refer to 'making something' out of tragedy, to turning suffering into something meaningful.

I've found meaning as a brain injury speaker, author, and the leader of Brain Injury Voices. This is my life's work. There are many ways to make meaning out of adversity. Here are some other possibilities to consider:

- Spending time with family and friends
- Volunteering
- Nurturing creativity through art, crafts, music or writing
- Helping someone
- Caring for an animal
- Tending a garden
- Devoting time to a spiritual practice.

It's about whatever brings a sense of purpose into your life. When you can make meaning out of all you've been through, the door to your new life is flung wide open.

Making it Your Own

Make Something: Create Meaning out of Suffering

What activity could you try to make meaning out of adversity?

- ☐ Spend time with family and friends
- ☐ Volunteer
- ☐ Make art
- ☐ Do crafts
- ☐ Create music
- ☐ Write about your experience
- ☐ Help someone
- ☐ Care for an animal
- ☐ Tend a garden
- ☐ Devote time to a spiritual practice

☐ Other _____

What meaning have you found in your brain injury?

_____

_____

_____

Conclusion

Finding another door of happiness is key to the brain injury acceptance process. Creating that new life is not something that happens overnight. It's a long process, one that often takes years. Know that you will grow and change as you progress through this journey. You will be in a different place one year, two years and five years from now. That's true of life in general, not just life with a brain injury.

Never give up on having a fulfilling life. Yes, brain injury means that dreams may have to change. But by getting to know your new self, listening for your inner wisdom, taking action, building on success, giving to others, taking risks and creating meaning, you can discover your personal door of happiness and acceptance.

Making it Your Own

Crafting a New Life

Which crafting a new life step had the most meaning for you?

- ☐ Get to know your new self
- ☐ Listen for the wisdom of the little voice inside
- ☐ Take action
- ☐ Start small, find success and build on it
- ☐ Find ways to give to others
- ☐ Take risks: Feel the fear and move forward anyway
- ☐ Make something: Create meaning out of suffering

Taking it Further

What's one thing you learned from reading this chapter?

_____

_____

_____

What action are you ready to take?

_____

_____

_____

Tracking your Progress

You may choose to answer the questions below periodically, as a way to track your progress over time.

What have you learned about your new self?

_____

_____

_____

Which way does your inner wisdom lead you?

_____

_____

_____

What actions, no matter how small, have you taken?

_____

_____

_____

What successes have you had?

_____

_____

_____

In what ways have you given to others?

_____

_____

_____

What risks have you taken?

_____

_____

_____

What meaning have you found in your experience so far?

_____

_____

_____

CHAPTER 9

The Brain Injury Portfolio: Documenting Progress, Pride & Purpose

Nothing builds self-esteem and self-confidence like accomplishment.

~Thomas Carlyle

One of the challenges of building a new life after brain injury is learning to like the new you. That challenge includes learning to stop comparing your pre-brain injury self to your post-brain injury self. Keeping a record of your progress and accomplishments is a strategy that can help you to stop comparing, accept and even embrace your new self. Rediscovering pride in what you <u>can</u> do moves you forward.

Learning to stop comparing was one of my most difficult lessons. In my mind, the new Carole created by brain injury could never measure up to the old Carole. The more comparing I did, the worse I felt about myself.

I had to learn to value the new me, not as a poor substitute for the old me, but as a valuable, worthwhile, accomplished person in her own right. Creating a *Stuff I'm Proud of* portfolio helped me do that. I hope the story of my portfolio will encourage you to start your own.

Lost in the Past

I've always enjoyed saving mementos and organizing them into scrapbooks. I like visual cues to remember my past and take pride in what I've done.

In my former life as a teacher, I kept a professional portfolio. It was a large three-ring binder which included documentation of all my teaching-related accomplishments. There were multiple sections for all the different classes I'd taught and the skills I'd developed as an educator.

For the first several years after my brain injury, I forgot all about my professional portfolio; I was more focused on relearning basic life tasks. One day, I came across the portfolio in the back of my desk drawer.

Reading it triggered the crushing grief I felt about my lost life. Every page documented the activities that the old me could do well and the new me couldn't do at all. I'd been a professional educator; now I felt like a professional patient.

The portfolio highlighted all the harsh judgments I then believed about the new me; I was inadequate, a failure and a cracked version of my former self who would never again achieve anything worthwhile.

Every day, I pulled out my portfolio and thought about all the losses. I compared the unwelcome new me, who I hated, to the accomplished old me, who I missed so much. The more I looked at my portfolio, the more devastated I felt. I knew it wasn't healthy to do, but I couldn't seem to stop myself. I'd gotten myself into a pattern that I couldn't break.

The 'Aha' Moment

Sometimes a jolt is needed to break an unhealthy cycle. My jolt came as a sudden moment of insight about a month later. This insight changed the way I thought about myself and my brain injury. It came from using a thought-stopping technique my counselor had given me.

The technique involved testing the truthfulness of my thoughts. The goal was to tame my tendency to judge myself so harshly and unfairly. I placed copies of the technique throughout my house, so I could re-member to use it in the moment.

One day, as I looked at my professional portfolio and sobbed over my lost life, I saw the thought stopping-technique on my desk. I asked myself, 'Is it true that I no longer have any accomplishments'? With a sudden jolt of awareness, I realized the answer to that question was a loud and clear 'no, not true'.

I did have accomplishments. Even though I could no longer do the activities documented in my portfolio, there were still multiple activi-ties that the new me had accomplished.

In my head, I started to list those activities. I had written a few poems, one of which was published on a brain injury website. I'd discovered a new, great satisfaction in using my hands to make crafts. I was volunteering for about thirty minutes a week at an organization where I used to work. With help from my Occupational Therapist, I had created a six week menu plan, which allowed me to regain control of my cooking.

Even though those accomplishments were very different from my previous ones, I realized that I was extremely proud of them. I thought that pride in myself was gone forever after my brain injury. It was, when I endlessly compared my old and new selves.

However, pride returned when I focused on what I'd accomplished as the new me. I realized that my post-brain injury successes deserved my recognition just as much as the ones from my previous life. Feelings of pride can be a powerful motivator.

A New Portfolio: Pride made Visible

Those feelings of pride in myself motivated me to create a new portfolio highlighting accomplishments since my brain injury. I took pictures of my crafts and printed copies of my poems, my 6-week meal plan and the volunteer project. Then my brain got overwhelmed by all the items. I didn't know what to do next.

At that time, I didn't have the organizational ability to categorize and compile those early accomplishments into a put-together portfolio. So, I took a nap and then put the project aside for a few days. Sometimes taking a break is what's needed to come up with a solution.

After a few days and discussions with family and friends, I came up with that solution. Since I couldn't create a portfolio, instead I put all the items in a manila folder on my desk. I called it the *Stuff I'm Proud of* folder. It was a simpler solution that gave me the same benefits as a portfolio.

Being able to see documentation of the accomplishments I was proud of all in one place helped me to feel better about the new me. Focusing on what <u>can</u> be done is a way to move forward.

Over time, I added more items to the *Stuff I'm Proud of* folder. It included more poems and pictures of crafts and other activities, volunteer recognition certificates, flyers and ticket stubs from events I attended and notes from talks I gave. My criteria for inclusion in the folder was any activity, large or small, that I was proud of or represented progress. Eventually, that folder bulged with many accomplishments.

A couple years later, I was asked to participate in a workshop about creativity after brain injury. I decided the workshop was the perfect opportunity to create a more formal portfolio. I purchased a large 3-ring binder, dividers and a box of sheet protectors.

Since I still struggled with organizational tasks, I asked for help. The Recreation Therapist at the outpatient brain injury clinic I attended helped me sort and divide the *Stuff I'm Proud of* folder into several sections—Writing, Crafts, Brain Injury Speaking, Volunteering and Other, for anything that didn't fit neatly into a category. Each section was organized with the earliest activities in the back and the most recent ones in the front.

Seeing my *Stuff I'm Proud of* folder put together into an organized portfolio gave me even more feelings of pride, satisfaction and accomplishment. I named this portfolio *After the Crash.*

Benefits of a Portfolio

After the Crash is a visual reminder of the progress I've made and the pride I feel in what I've achieved since my brain injury. It's rewarding to compare the early activities in the back to the more recent ones in the front. Many once challenging activities are now easy for me. During times when I feel sad, and all I can see is what I can't do, my portfolio shows me just how far I've come and the pride I have in my accomplishments.

As I've documented my small successes gradually building into larger ones, I've stopped comparing the new me to who I was before my brain injury. My former professional portfolio now lives in a box in my attic, one that I haven't opened for many years. In fact, I also now look at my pre-brain injury life as a box that I store inside me, but no longer need to open.

Paying attention to what I'm proud of now keeps me centered in the present moment, not lost in the past. Instead of focusing on the way life used to be, I put my energies into continuing to create this new life.

After the Crash reminds me that the way forward after brain injury is to focus on what I can do and build from there. As of this writing, I've been adding items to my portfolio for nearly fifteen years. It's now four inches thick!

Tips to Create a Portfolio

If you would like to begin your own portfolio, here's some advice based on my experience:

- *Start with a Stuff I'm Proud of folder.* Don't attempt to categorize anything at first. The most important task is to put stuff in the folder.
- *Think about what you're proud of since your brain injury.* Ask family, friends or medical professionals for help if needed. Here are some examples to get you thinking:
  - A strategy you've learned
  - An activity you did that you thought you couldn't do
  - Something you tried for the first time
  - A task you've mastered
  - Places you've gone
  - Anything you've created
  - Successes you've had
  - Lessons you've learned
- *Figure out how to document what you're proud of.* That may include:
  - Mementos from places you go
  - Pictures of things you're proud of
  - Copies or pictures of things you've created
  - Notes and cards you receive
  - Progress reports from your medical team
- *Write a brief note with each item explaining how it represents progress or why you're proud of it.* This will help you remember the stories behind what you've saved.
- *Date each item.*

- *If you decide to turn your Stuff I'm Proud of folder into a portfolio, you may want to ask someone for help.* Sorting and categorizing can be challenging tasks.
- *Continue adding items to your folder or portfolio.* Seeing your accomplishments multiply will be very rewarding!

A portfolio can help you to accept and like your new self after brain injury. I hope you'll think about all that you've accomplished since your brain injury and begin your own *Stuff I'm Proud of* folder.

Making it Your Own

The Brain Injury Portfolio

What have you accomplished since your brain injury? Here are some possibilities to consider:

☐ I learned this strategy_____

☐ I did this activity_____

☐ I tried this thing for the first time_____

☐ I mastered this task_____

☐ I went to this place_____

☐ I created this thing_____

☐ I had this success_____

☐ I learned this lesson_____

Other Accomplishments: _____

_____

How can you document those accomplishments?

_____

_____

_____

Taking it Further

What's one thing you learned from reading this chapter?

_____

_____

_____

What action are you ready to take?

_____

_____

_____

CHAPTER 10

Transforming Grief: Coping with Brain Injury Anniversary Day

Keep your face always toward the sunshine and the shadows will fall behind you.

~Walt Whitman

Feelings of loss after brain injury can show up at unexpected times. Even when you've mostly come to terms with your new life, grief may still get triggered. One time when grief can increase is around the anniversary date of your brain injury. It's the day that sharply and forever divides your life into a before and an after.

Part of acceptance is recognizing grief triggers and finding strategies to cope with them. This is how I've transformed my brain injury anniversary date from a time of mourning to a time of reflection and even celebration.

Recognizing Anniversary Day Grief

I used to dread July 6th, the anniversary day of my brain injury. For many years, beginning every early June, I would start remembering and grieving more acutely my life that was. I would think a lot about what I was doing in the weeks before my life changed forever. In June of 1999, I was juggling free-lance teaching jobs and a grant writing project. I was busy with musical activities: orchestra, chorale and a small part in an upcoming musical. I was looking forward to traveling to England to visit my college roommate later that summer.

The more that I thought about my pre-brain injury life, the more intensely I grieved all that I'd lost. I missed being able to manage and excel at many activities. Even when I had processed a lot of my brain injury grief, it still seemed to rush back on me at anniversary time. I relentlessly compared myself to the old Carole. The new Carole always came up short. My ongoing brain injury symptoms and limitations frustrated me even more. I got angry at myself because I hadn't progressed further. In the process, I discounted all the gains I'd made. I needed a strategy to cope with the extra feelings of sadness and loss brought on by my brain injury anniversary date.

The Brain Injury Anniversary Strategy

It took me eight anniversaries and the help of family and friends to come up with a strategy that worked for July 6th. It's one that I use every year now. This strategy has transformed anniversary time from a day of intense sadness to a day I enjoy. I now view my anniversary day as my second birthday and commemorate it as such. The anniversary strategy involves four important components:

- Don't be alone
- Recognize and celebrate your progress
- Plan life-affirming activities
- Try something new

Don't be Alone

It's never a good idea to be all alone on such a meaningful day. When alone, it's very easy to allow yourself to brood about what was your life. Instead, it's more helpful to spend time with an upbeat person or persons who understands the challenges of anniversary day and can treat you with empathy, not pity.

The last thing you need—on anniversary day or any other day—is a boatload of pity, such as 'Oh you poor dear, I feel so sorry for you.' While pity may feel helpful at first, ultimately it will only deepen your feelings of grief, leaving you stuck in the past. In contrast, empathy is all about offering support, encouragement and understanding. Receiving empathy on anniversary day can uplift you.

Recognize and Celebrate your Progress

It's easy to forget the progress you've made since your brain injury, especially around anniversary time. It may seem like what you can do now is not very much. As you move forward, it's not fair to judge your new life by the standards of your old one. That kind of judgment will only make anniversary time more painful.

However, if you compare your current abilities to what you were like early on after your brain injury, then it's easier to see all the gains you've made. It doesn't matter whether those gains are big ones or small ones. Every bit of improvement you make deserves to be recognized. When you pay attention to your progress, anniversary time can become less a time to mourn and more a time to celebrate just how far you've come.

Plan Life-Affirming Activities

It's important to think about how you'd like to spend your anniversary day. Planning and doing something fun and fulfilling serves two purposes. The planning process itself can distract you during the days or weeks before the actual anniversary and give you something to look forward to. A life-affirming activity on the day itself will prevent you from thinking too much about your pre-injury life.

Whatever activity you choose, it should fill your soul and respect your current abilities. The last thing you want is to choose something too difficult that will frustrate and depress you. Depending on your abilities and endurance, you may plan one activity or several. You may require help planning or you may be able to do it on your own. Perhaps you'd like to spend time with several people or maybe just one. You may even choose to pursue a solo activity. Just be sure not to spend all day alone.

Regarding the type of activity, there is no right or wrong choice. It should be life-affirming to you. Listen to the wisdom of your inner voice for guidance. Here are some possibilities to consider:

- Spending time with family or friends
- Doing a craft/art project
- Volunteering
- Gardening
- Reading to a child
- Listening to/playing music
- Spending time in nature
- Cooking a special meal
- Building something
- Playing with a pet
- Exercising

Try Something New

This is my favorite part of the anniversary day strategy. Do something you've never done before. Since you began a new life with your brain injury, anniversary day should be commemorated by trying something new. The life-affirming activity and the new activity may be one in the same, but they don't have to be.

The activity doesn't need to be long or complicated, just new. For example, the first year I implemented this strategy, I went with friends to a restaurant and ordered a dish I'd never eaten before. Over the years, my new activities have gotten bigger as my capabilities have expanded. It's most important to try something that's in line with whatever your current abilities are. So unless you're truly up for it, I wouldn't recommend any activity that's too challenging.

What the activity represents is far more important than the activity itself. As with the life-affirming strategy, planning and doing something new can serve as a distraction and give you something to look forward to.

Over the years, July 6th has been a day when I've gone to the botanical gardens with my best friend, created collages with my brain injury support group, watched a rubber duck race, ridden a gondola up a mountain, hiked to a waterfall with my family, taken pictures at the beach and eaten many more new foods.

I never would have dreamed it early on, but I can honestly say that I now enjoy July 6th. Yes, I will always know that it's the day brain injury changed my life forever. However, with the help of my strategy, it's been transformed into a positive, celebratory, forward-looking day. I hope the anniversary strategy can help you do the same.

Making it Your Own

Transforming Grief

How do you feel before/on the anniversary of your brain injury?

_____

_____

_____

What strategies have you used to deal with those feelings?

_____

_____

_____

_____

Who would you like to spend your brain injury anniversary day with?

_____

_____

What can you do now that you couldn't do early on after your brain injury?

_____

_____

_____

What life-affirming activity could you do on anniversary day?

- ☐ Spend time with family or friends
- ☐ Do a craft/art project
- ☐ Volunteer
- ☐ Garden
- ☐ Read to a child
- ☐ Listen to/play music
- ☐ Spend time in nature
- ☐ Cook a special meal
- ☐ Build something
- ☐ Play with a pet
- ☐ Exercise
- ☐ Other_____

What's a doable activity that you've never done before that you can try on brain injury anniversary day?

_____

_____

Taking it Further

What's one thing you learned from reading this chapter?

_____

_____

_____

What action are you ready to take?

_____

_____

_____

CHAPTER 11

Oh, The Things People Say

It is not the mountain we conquer, but ourselves.

~Sir Edmund Hillary

Coping with brain injury symptoms takes every ounce of determination, courage and patience we possess. On top of that already steep challenge, most of us are also subjected to many unwelcome comments about our injuries. These comments can range from well-meaning to ignorant to judgmental to downright mean. Whatever the intention, they often sting like salt in an open wound.

When you're moving as fast as you can just to stay upright, one comment can be enough to knock you off course. Words drop like bombs on an already fragile psyche. These word bombs can come from family, friends, medical professionals, the general public and even complete strangers. It's especially devastating when they come from the people closest to you or the professionals you look to for guidance.

One hallmark of brain injury acceptance is when those comments no longer have so much power over you. Strategies can help you deal with the words that hurt.

Words that Hurt

Have you heard statements like these?

- *You look fine to me.*
- *Oh, that happens to me too! At least you can blame it on brain injury.*
- *I know someone who had a brain injury and he/she is just fine now.*
- *Aren't you back to work yet?*
- *I wish I could take a nap every day. Aren't you lucky!*
- *It could have been worse!*
- *Oh come on, just push through it and you'll be fine. Don't be lazy.*
- *Maybe you're depressed.*
- *You're just getting older.*
- *Stop using your brain injury as an excuse.*
- *You talk about your brain injury too much.*

I've heard multiple variations of every one of those statements. They were crushing to me, especially during my first few years as a brain injury survivor. I already felt very alone in my injury. Statements like those increased how isolated I felt. So many people didn't seem to understand the life-shaking magnitude of what I was going through. Their words often minimized my symptoms or seemed to express doubt that they were even real. Every comment, even the well-meaning ones, felt like an attack on my sense of self, and on who I was as a person.

Because my sense of self was damaged by my brain injury and very fragile, I had little ability to cope with the comments. I wanted to speak out, but I didn't have the language. I couldn't explain why I was so hurt. Most of the time, I just smiled weakly at whomever made the comment. However, inside I was devastated. Sometimes I'd cry for hours over a particular comment. There were a few that took me years to recover from.

It didn't help that my injury was invisible. I looked fine. Sometimes I almost wished for a cane, a brace, a scar—anything to make my struggles more apparent and thus more real to others. Now I know that nothing would have stopped the comments. They're part of what we deal with as brain injury survivors. Comments that hurt seem to be an unfortunate part of any loss that's misunderstood by others.

Finding your Power

The way I see it, there's good news and bad news about words that hurt. Here's the bad news first. Unfortunately, there's little we can do to stop people's unwelcome comments. Their brains and mouths are not within our control. You'll probably hear some comments that leave you speechless. Sometimes they'll come from the people you depend on. It's small comfort, but know that most of the time, people say hurtful things out of lack of knowledge, not malice. Unless they've lived it, the life-shattering impact of brain injury symptoms and subsequent loss of self are next to impossible for people to understand.

The good news is that there are strategies to help you cope with those comments. You don't have to be emotionally held hostage by other people's words. None of these strategies is a quick fix. I wish I could wave a magic wand and then *Poof!* You're no longer affected by what people say. Unfortunately, it doesn't seem to work that way. Like everything with brain injury, it's a process. The stronger your new sense of self becomes, the less the comments people make will bother you.

Depending on where you are in your brain injury journey, that may sound impossible. I would have thought that during the early years of my own journey, when I was devastated by people's comments. Back then, getting people to stop saying words that hurt me seemed like the best strategy. Sometimes that worked, but not often. We can't always rely on people to say the right thing. That puts our emotional well-being outside of us, in the hands of others.

I want us to focus on what we can control. The only person we have any control of in this situation is ourselves. That's where our power is. The greater your own inner power, the less power others—and their words—will have over you.

I never would have imagined it early on, but I can now honestly say that the comments don't bother me anymore. It's not that I don't still hear them. I do. Just recently, someone at an event said to me, 'But you don't look like you have a brain injury'. What they couldn't see or know is that I'd spent the better part of the day resting on my couch in order to build up enough mental energy to attend that event.

In the past, that kind of comment would leave me teary at best, angry at worst. Now, it doesn't bring out any emotional reaction other than mild amusement. So what's different? The comments aren't different. I am different. I have a strong sense of self again. I know who I am as a brain injury survivor. That sense of self is kind of like an inoculation against the devastation of words that hurt.

Strategies to Cope

Here's a list of strategies that gradually helped me develop that immunity. They range from self-protection to self-advocacy. Not every strategy applies to every situation, so take what works for you.

- Be gentle with yourself
- Learn about your brain injury
- Work on not taking the comments personally
- Be careful who you talk to and how much you share about your brain injury
- Limit your contact with certain people
- Talk to other brain injury survivors
- Use affirmations to counteract words that hurt
- Analyze why the comment bothers you and the intent behind it
- Write a script responding to words that hurt
- Develop empathy for some people who make unwelcome comments
- Look at the comments as an opportunity for education and advocacy

Be Gentle with Yourself

It's normal to feel hurt by unwelcome comments, especially when you're already fragile. It's ok that you often won't know how to respond. Acknowledge the hurt you feel and that you're doing the best you can. Continue to focus on getting to know the new you. Strengthening your new self takes time.

Learn about your Brain Injury

The better you understand your symptoms, the better able you will be to recognize when people's comments are just plain wrong. Knowledge is power.

Work on Not Taking the Comments Personally

I know, this one is easier said than done. Recognize that much of what people say is a reflection of them—their lack of knowledge about brain injury, their lack of empathy or their discomfort with another's hardships. The comments are not a reflection of you or your character. Other people's words do not define you.

Be Careful Who you Talk to and How Much you Share about your Brain Injury

The vast majority of people won't understand brain injury and will make unwelcome comments out of that ignorance. Keeping it 'close to the vest' can protect you from those comments while you're fragile.

Limit your Contact with Certain People

Some people in your life may be unable or unwilling to understand brain injury. They may continue to use words that hurt, no matter what you say. Sometimes, for your own self-protection, you have to limit the time you spend with them.

Talk to Other Brain Injury Survivors

There's often an instant rapport among survivors, because we 'get it'. We've all been subjected to numerous unwelcome comments and can offer empathy like no one else can. We can also learn to laugh about the comments together. It's helpful to know that we're not alone.

Use Affirmations to Counteract Words that Hurt

Affirmations are short, positive statements. They're words you can say to yourself or write down to read. They should be statements that you can believe. The idea behind affirmations is that repeating them over and over gets them into your consciousness. They can help you see yourself in a more positive light. Here are a few examples: 'I'm doing the best I can', 'I'm moving forward at my own pace', 'I don't give up', 'I'm learning to like my new self'.

Analyze Why the Comment Bothers you and The Intent Behind It

What is it about the comment that pushes your buttons? Does the comment show the person's ignorance about brain injury? Are you being judged unfairly? Does the comment minimize your brain injury symptoms? Does it doubt that your brain injury is real? Does the comment try to compare your brain injury symptoms to the normal life challenges that everyone faces?

When you understand the reason behind why a comment upsets you, you can begin to figure out the appropriate response to it. You can also look behind it. What was the intent of the comment? Was someone trying to help you but just phrased it badly? Is there any-thing useful you can take from the comment that will help you?

Write a Script Responding to Words that Hurt

One of the challenges is that comments often leave us speechless. Writing and rehearsing a short script for how you'd like to respond to certain comments can help you be more prepared. It may feel awk-ward at first, but the more you use it, the easier it gets.

The script isn't about insulting the other person for their comment. That won't help the situation. Here are a few options for starting your script. 'When you say _____, I feel _____' or 'When you say _____, this is the message I hear_____'. 'Here's what I wish you'd say instead_____'.

If writing the script is difficult for you, ask for help from a person you trust. The more you practice your script, the more likely you'll be able to remember and use it in the moment.

Develop Empathy for Some People who Make Unwelcome Comments

We'd like the people closest to us to understand brain injury in the same way we do, at the same time. However, they may be a few steps behind us, especially early on. While helping us on our brain injury journey, they're also going through a journey of their own. They also feel sad, scared, confused and frustrated. Their lives have been changed by brain injury too. Often they're doing the best they can to cope, and sometimes they say the wrong thing. Give them time to catch up.

Look at the Comments as an Opportunity for Education and Advocacy.

When your sense of self is strong enough, unwelcome comments become teachable moments. They give you the chance to educate others about brain injury and to advocate for what you need. As individuals with disabilities, we're the best people to help others understand our challenges. One person at a time, we can work to correct the many misperceptions about brain injury.

It's not fair that we have to cope with all the challenges of brain injury and with words that hurt at the same time. With time and strategies, the sting from unwelcome comments can fade. As acceptance takes root, it gets easier to advocate for yourself and move forward with your new life.

Making it Your Own

Oh, The Things People Say

What comments have people said to you about brain injury?

- ☐ You look fine to me.
- ☐ Oh, that happens to me too! At least you can blame it on brain injury.
- ☐ I know someone who had a brain injury and he/she is just fine now.
- ☐ Aren't you back to work yet?
- ☐ I wish I could take a nap every day. Aren't you lucky!
- ☐ It could have been worse!
- ☐ Oh come on, just push through it and you'll be fine. Don't be lazy.
- ☐ Maybe you're depressed.
- ☐ You're just getting older.
- ☐ Stop using your brain injury as an excuse.
- ☐ You talk about your brain injury too much.

Other comments you've heard:_____

_____

_____

_____

Which strategies are most helpful for you right now?

☐ Be gentle with yourself
☐ Learn about your brain injury
☐ Work on not taking the comments personally
☐ Be careful who you talk to and how much you share about your brain injury
☐ Limit your contact with certain people
☐ Talk to other brain injury survivors
☐ Use affirmations to counteract words that hurt
☐ Analyze why the comment bothers you and the intent behind it
☐ Write a script responding to words that hurt
☐ Develop empathy for some people who make unwelcome comments
☐ Look at the comments as an opportunity for education and advocacy

What unwelcome comment bothers you the most?

_____

_____

Write an affirmation that could help you cope with that unwelcome comment. See pages 69 and 133 for examples of affirmations.

_____

_____

_____

Write a script for what you can say the next time you hear that comment.

- When you say _____

  I feel _____

- When you say _____

  this is the message I hear_____

- Here's what I wish you'd say instead_____

  _____

Taking it Further

What's one thing you learned from reading this chapter?

_____

_____

_____

What action are you ready to take?

_____

_____

_____

CHAPTER 12

In a Different Light:
The Power of Humor

Humor is tragedy plus time.

~Mark Twain

Humor is an age-old strategy for coping with adversity. When life is falling apart and out of our control, sometimes all we can do is laugh. Being able to find humor in brain injury is helpful on the journey toward acceptance and moving forward with a new life.

I learned about the power of humor from my mentor, Bev Bryant. Bev was a brain injury survivor, author and national speaker. She loved to put jokes in her speeches and used them to make important points. Here's one from her talk *Humor in Healing*. It's a joke best read aloud to appreciate the punchline, and the content is for adults.

One morning, a 90-year-old grandfather heard a knock on the door, and when he opened it, there stood a voluptuous woman dressed in black lingerie and high heels. She leaned over and whispered to him. 'I'm here to give you super sex!' Without hesitating, he leaned right back and said 'Thank you. I'll take the soup.'

After the audience had finished laughing, Bev made her point: 'We always have the right to choose, not just between soup or sex....but what we are going to do with the rest of our lives. We may not be able to change what has happened, but we can always change how we deal with it...Humor is about a state of being...It's about seeing things and events in a different light and from a different perspective.'

When I first met Bev about a year after my brain injury, I was horrified by how she would laugh and make jokes about her own brain injury symptoms. I would think 'How can she do that? Brain injury is very sad; it's not funny'. At the time, I didn't think I could ever find humor in my brain injury. But both Mark Twain and Bev Bryant were right; over time, I did begin to view my symptoms in a more lighthearted way.

Bev taught me that finding humor is a choice. Eventually, you get to the point where you can either continue to cry about what's happened or you can just laugh.

Laughter is a healthy choice we can make for ourselves. Laughing about brain injury can reduce stress, both in the body and mind. When we can laugh, we heal psychologically. When we can laugh, we are resilient.

Humor is like WD-40; it's the grease that makes everything move more smoothly. Humor doesn't change all the challenges of brain injury, but it can make them more bearable. As Nazi concentration camp survivor Victor Frankl said, 'What helps people survive awful circumstances is their ability to detach and get beyond themselves. This is seen in heroism and humor.'

How do you get to the humor? It's about reframing the situation and renaming the experience, or as Bev said, looking at things in a different light and from a different perspective.

I began my humor journey by naming my brain injury. I wanted a lighthearted way to describe it, something that would make me and others laugh. Often it seems like there are two very different people living in my head—me and my brain injury. My brain injury is a diva. She's the one in charge who gets what she wants when she wants it. So, I gave her a dramatic name—Brainhilda. My family, friends and medical team are all very familiar with Brainhilda and her antics. Naming my injury was a way to distance myself from the brain injury, to know that I was not my injury. Doing that helped me to find the humor in my symptoms.

Over the years, I've continued to find more humor in Brainhilda. Most of my humor centers on my mental fatigue and how much and how often I need to rest. For example, one day I told my doctor that I've had so much beauty sleep over the years that one of these days, I'm going to wake up as a supermodel!

Due to my mental fatigue, I've also had to nap in many locations. When Brainhilda says nap, I must obey, no matter where I am. Some of my odder resting locations have included a classroom in a craft store, the coffin display room at a funeral home (I rested on a couch, not in a coffin!), the bedding department at a furniture store, a hotel bar (I hadn't been drinking and the sign did say Bar and Lounge!), a golf course pro shop and the Washington, DC conference room of a U.S. senator. Given all that, I like to tell people that I sleep around!

My motto is one that Star Trek fans will appreciate—*To boldly nap where no one has napped before!*

Humor has helped bridge the gap between me and people without brain injuries. When I can laugh and joke about my symptoms, it puts others at ease. I feel less of a divide between myself and others.

But what if you're just not there yet? What if you're where I was when I first met Bev Bryant and the idea of brain injury humor seems impossible and maybe kind of appalling? Here are a few suggestions:

- *Give yourself some more time.* It may just be too soon for humor for you. But know that it can come and be open to the possibility.
- *Talk to other survivors who are further along in their journey.* Those who have found ways to laugh at themselves and their injuries can be good role models. Their humor can rub off on you.
- *When brain injury symptoms make you sad or frustrated, ask your-self, 'Is there another way to look at this?'* That question can encourage you to find not only humor, but also gratitude and silver linings within brain injury.
- *Find other ways to laugh*—funny movies, comedy routines, jokes, comic strips, the antics of children and/or pets.

Finding humor takes time and courage. I encourage you to look for ways to laugh about brain injury. Choose to be amused.

Making it Your Own

The Power of Humor

If you were to choose a name for your brain injury, what would it be?

_____

_____

What brain injury symptom would you like to find humor in?

_____

How could you view that symptom in a different light or from a different perspective? Here's one example:

- Memory Challenges: I can wrap my own presents and still be surprised when I open them!

_____

_____

_____

Taking it Further

What's one thing you learned from reading this chapter?

_____

_____

_____

What action are you ready to take?

_____

_____

_____

CHAPTER 13

A Glimmer of Good:
Finding Silver Linings

Since the house is on fire, let us warm ourselves.

~Italian Proverb

I've always been a big believer in the concept of silver linings—that some good can come from adversity, that it's possible to find meaning in suffering. Brain injury put that belief to its biggest test ever. It's so challenging to find silver linings in something as life-consuming as brain injury. It's much easier to list all of brain injury's negative consequences. They are very numerous, very real, and turn our lives upside down and inside out.

Over the years, I've cried buckets of tears and grieved deeply the loss of my old life and my sense of self. I don't like having a disability and the limitations that come with it. But yes, even within something as devastating as brain injury, there can be silver linings.

The Value of Silver Linings

Without silver linings, the pain of coping with brain injury can become all-consuming. Finding silver linings gives you power—the power to see the positive, the power to assert some small measure of control in a situation that's mostly out of your control, the power to find meaning and move forward with a new life.

More and more psychological research is being done about the benefits of being able to find the positive within the negative. There are studies showing that people who can find silver linings within tragedy are more resilient, have a lower incidence of depression and post-traumatic stress disorder and better health overall.

Finding Silver Linings

It took me several years to find the silver linings in my brain injury. At first, all I had to hold on to was the belief that they were there, even if I couldn't see them yet. To be honest, there were times when my belief in the possibility of silver linings was one of the things that kept me from ending my life. I had to believe that some good could come from all I was going through. So, if you're in the place where you can't see how there could be any silver linings to brain injury, please have faith that you can find them; you will find them.

Silver linings don't have to be big and life altering. Often they start out as quite small. But that doesn't mean insignificant. Every silver lining has power and the more you find, the more powerful you become.

My very first silver lining started out as a half-hearted joke. Because brain injury has dulled my sense of smell somewhat, I can now chop onions without crying. One day when visiting at my parent's house, I noticed my mother was tearing up as she chopped onions. I joked that even though brain injury had made me pretty much useless at most things, here was a task I could succeed at. Yes, I insulted myself, as I did a lot back then, but buried within that was a silver lining. I could chop onions without crying. I could be useful in some small way.

That silver lining led to a new role for me preparing family dinners. I was the designated onion chopper. I didn't recognize it then, but looking back now, I realize that was an early step in using silver linings to move forward. Silver linings helped me to focus on what I could do and to find new avenues of success.

I think of silver linings as being on one half of a balance scale, with brain injury being the enormous load on the other side. We need something to counterbalance the downward weight of brain injury. Of course, my first silver lining of realizing I could be helpful chopping onions did nothing to budge the mental, physical, emotional and spiritual burden of brain injury. However, it opened the door to finding more silver linings.

Ever so gradually, as I added more silver linings to the scale, the brain injury weight began to lighten and I started to move forward with my new life. The more I focused on the good that had come from my brain injury, the better I felt about myself. Here's a list of some of my silver linings. I'm sharing them in the hope that they encourage you to think of your own.

- Because of brain injury, I understand what it is to struggle and I've become a better person for it. I have more empathy, compassion, perception and wisdom.

- Because of brain injury, I've become less of a perfectionist. I was always a hard driving, Type A personality. I'm now gentler with myself, more tolerant of my own mistakes and the mistakes of others. I'm more relaxed and able to live in the present moment.

- Because of brain injury, I've discovered strength I didn't know I had. Coming through the brain injury grief and loss of self gives me tremendous confidence in my own resilience.

- Because of brain injury, my relationships have deepened. Even though some people drifted away after my brain injury, I grew closer to the family members and friends who remained. I hug them every time we meet, because I know how precious they are. I've learned to accept their help and to help them in the ways I'm able.

- Because of brain injury, I have a clearer sense of purpose in my life. Although I can no longer work full or even part-time, I've found my life's work—helping others with brain injuries as an educator, advocate, mentor, speaker and writer. Brain injury gave me the passion for a cause that I was missing.

Reading that list of silver linings, it may sound like brain injury was the best thing that ever happened to me. It wasn't. It was the worst. Silver linings are not meant to gloss over the physical, mental, emotional and spiritual devastation that accompany brain injury. No amount of silver linings will change the fact that brain injury is extremely challenging to cope with. The trick to living successfully with brain injury is to not get permanently stuck in all its awfulness. Silver linings can take some of the sting out of brain injury, give us something else to focus on and thus help us move forward in our journey.

Silver Lining Strategies

How do you find the silver linings in your brain injury? The first step is to believe they exist. The next step is to make a conscious effort to look for the positive within the negative. Think of finding silver linings like a muscle that needs to be strengthened. The more you use it, the better you'll get at it.

Here are some questions you can ask yourself to uncover potential positives within the negative that is brain injury:

- How has brain injury made me a stronger person?
- How has brain injury made me a better person?
- How has brain injury improved my relationships?
- Who are the people I've met because of my brain injury?
- What opportunities have I had because of my brain injury?
- How has my brain injury influenced what's most important to me in life?
- How has brain injury changed my sense of purpose in life?

Brain injury takes so much from us. Find the glimmer of good in it, no matter how small or insignificant it may seem. That can change your focus from looking backward to looking forward. Acceptance won't happen until that switch is made. I encourage you to believe in and look for your silver linings.

Making it Your Own

Finding Silver Linings

Which silver lining question resonates most strongly for you?

- ☐ How has brain injury made me a stronger person?
- ☐ How has brain injury made me a better person?
- ☐ How has brain injury improved my relationships?
- ☐ Who are the people I've met because of my brain injury?
- ☐ What opportunities have I had because of my brain injury?
- ☐ How has my brain injury influenced what's most important to me in life?
- ☐ How has brain injury changed my sense of purpose in life?

- ☐ Other question_____

What's your answer to the question you chose?

_____

_____

_____

Based on your answer to the question above, write your own brain injury silver lining statements. See page 148 for examples.

- ▪ Because of brain injury, _____

_____

- Because of brain injury, _____

_____

- Because of brain injury, _____

_____

How do your silver linings influence how you feel about your brain injury?

_____

_____

Taking it Further

What's one thing you learned from reading this chapter?

_____

_____

_____

What action are you ready to take?

_____

_____

_____

CHAPTER 14

Choosing Gratitude

Gratitude bestows reverence...changing forever how we experience life and the world.

~John Milton

Brain injury launches us into a swirling, dark world. We may be angry about what's happened to us; grieving what we've lost; worrying about what will become of us; frustrated as we try to navigate the complexity of everyday life with a brain that doesn't work the same anymore. Sometimes it feels like our past, present and future have been sacrificed to this horrible injury. Acceptance of all these issues is a steep hill to climb. How can you find your footing when so much has been stripped away?

It doesn't seem possible, but expressing gratitude is a strategy that may help you find your way through all that darkness. Yes, gratitude. Believe me, I get it—when your life has been devastated by brain injury, being grateful is probably the last thing on your mind. However, gratitude can be a powerful tool in your journey toward accepting brain injury. My experience has been that gratitude can be most helpful when life is at its worst.

Defining Gratitude

Expressing gratitude is about a lot more than saying thanks. It's about cultivating a deep appreciation of what's happening right now and paying attention to life's small moments that often pass by us unnoticed. Doing that can ground you in the present and give you something solid to hold on to as you inch your way forward.

Let's begin with a brief experiment. I invite you to think about the fill-in-the-blank statements below. You may choose to answer them silently on your own, discuss them in a group or write down your responses. Do whatever works best for you. I encourage you to take whatever time you need to come up with your answers.

Today I'm grateful for:

- This person in my life _____

- This item in my home_____

- This simple pleasure I enjoy_____

- This thing that made me smile or laugh_____

After answering those questions, how do you feel? Take a minute to check in with yourself and pay attention to what's happening to you physically, mentally and emotionally.

Gratitude has the power to affect us in body, mind and spirit. I've observed that when I think about what I'm grateful for, I feel my muscles relaxing, a smile growing and a lightness rising inside me.

Benefits of Gratitude

A lot of scientific research has been done on the physical, mental and emotional benefits of regularly expressing gratitude. Those benefits can include lower blood pressure; less pain; decreased depression, anxiety and loneliness; a stronger immune system; better sleep; increased self-esteem; greater happiness and more overall resilience against adversity.

What Gratitude Isn't

Gratitude almost sounds like a wonder drug, right? Who wouldn't want all those benefits? However, I wonder if some of you could be feeling a bit resistant to gratitude. Perhaps you're thinking something like this: 'Brain injury has left my life in shambles—how can I be grateful for anything?!'

Here's the first thing to know about gratitude. It doesn't mean that you have to feel thankful all the time and for everything. I'll be the first to admit that I don't always feel grateful. Sometimes I get lost in all the awfulness of brain injury too.

Gratitude also doesn't mean ignoring all the feelings we have about our brain injuries. As survivors, we have every reason to feel and safely express our sadness, anger, fear and any other emotions we may be experiencing.   Working through those feelings is part of acceptance too. Brain injury is a life-changing event of the highest magnitude, one that comes with a boatload of emotions. If you or other people try to push aside or cover up those emotions, they don't go away; they often get stronger.

Perhaps you've felt shamed into gratitude by statements like these: 'You should count your blessings' or 'You should be grateful for what you have.' Whenever the word 'should' is said or implied, beware! Guilt trip ahead!

Whenever I heard statements like those, here's the message I heard: 'You should just get over being sad, angry and scared about your brain injury. Gratitude is the fix you need.' If only it was that easy. It felt like gratitude was being offered as a glib, quick-fix answer to a much more complicated problem. I recognized that people were genuinely trying to help me and that the guilt trip message was unintentional, but it still made me feel worse about myself.

A Model of Gratitude

If gratitude isn't about trying to ignore emotions and putting an impossibly sunny face on brain injury, then what is it? I think of gratitude as a *both/and* concept rather than an *either/or* one. I know, that was a mouthful of a sentence. Bear with me while I explain what I mean. These concepts are an important part of making gratitude work for us.

If we think about gratitude as *either/or*, then we're <u>either</u> devastated by how brain injury has changed our lives <u>or</u> we're grateful for what we have. This 'one or the other' thinking reduces brain injury and gratitude to a simple choice between the two. We all know it's not that black and white.

I think *both/and* is a more useful way to think about gratitude. It's possible to be <u>both</u> devastated by brain injury <u>and</u> to find things to be grateful for. This model doesn't try to gloss over the tremendous challenges of brain injury. It honors all of our very real emotions and opens the door to the benefits of gratitude.

Ultimately, gratitude is a choice, a choice you make for yourself. It's about choosing to find something to be thankful for, even within the midst of the darkest of feelings. It's about believing that you can find gifts in your experience, even when life is at its worst. It's about letting sadness, anger and fear have their place, but making the conscious decision to turn away from them, at least for a short time, to focus on gratitude. It's about finding a way to live with the harsh reality of brain injury symptoms.

In my own journey, I struggled to cope with the sadness, anger and fear I felt after my brain injury. Even with professionals helping me, the overwhelming emotions I felt seemed to have no end to them. So much of my life felt out of my control. Whenever I focused on the big, 'how can I ever learn to live with brain injury?' thoughts, I just got overwhelmed by the sadness, anger and fear.

Over time, I learned that I felt better when I focused on things I could control, no matter how small they were. Gratitude was one of those things.

Keys to Making Gratitude Work

I've identified the following three strategies that helped make gratitude work for me:

- Focus on the small and specific
- Keep it fresh
- Make it a practice

Focus on the Small and Specific

The first key to unlocking gratitude was to focus my attention on something very small and very specific. No matter how bad life was, I could usually find something small and specific to be grateful for.

Sometimes I focused on being grateful for my immediate surroundings—the sun coming in my window, the soothing feeling of a warm cup of tea in my hands or the softness of the blanket I used at naptime.

Sometimes I focused on being grateful for the help I received from family and friends—the meals offered when I admitted my cooking challenges, the rides home when I got myself stranded due to brain injury fatigue, or the many times people talked me down when I called them confused and unsure what to do.

Sometimes I focused on being grateful for the small improvements I was making with help from medical professionals—being able to cook my own meals again, being able to enjoy a concert using earplugs and headphones, or being less overwhelmed in busy environments thanks to prism glasses.

The more I focused on small, specific things, the less hold the sadness, anger and fear had on me. I felt more empowered, less like a victim. It was as if gratitude took some of the power out of all those emotions, if only for a little while.

Did gratitude work all the time? No. Especially early on, it didn't take much to plunge me back into the depths of sadness, anger and fear. However, over time, as my gratitude list grew longer, I grew stronger. Gratitude is a muscle that needs regular exercise to reach its full potential.

Keep it Fresh

The second key to making gratitude work was to continue finding new things to be grateful for. Otherwise, gratitude risked becoming stale and losing its power. What we're extremely grateful for today can be what we take for granted tomorrow. For example, yes, I'm grateful I survived my car accident. However, I've been a survivor since 1999, so that gratitude has lost its immediacy. Gratitude for a long ago event doesn't usually evoke the same feelings as gratitude for a more recent event. Gratitude is most powerful when it's related to something current.

Make it a Practice

The third key to making gratitude work was to practice it regularly. There are many ways to express gratitude. I often used a notebook to write down what I was grateful for, so I could go back to it when I was feeling down. Sometimes I also silently made a list in my head, as a form of meditation. Here are some suggestions for ways to tap into gratitude:

- Write about what you're grateful for in a journal
- Meditate—either out loud or silently—about what you're grateful for
- Use a gratitude jar—write down what you're grateful for and put the slips of paper in a jar. Over time, watch the number of slips grow.
- Go around the table at dinner and ask each person to share what they're grateful for
- Write a letter to a person you're grateful for—you may choose to send it or keep it private
- Spend time in nature and look for things to be grateful for
- Cut out pictures and words from magazines and create a gratitude collage
- Set a daily alarm—when it goes off, think of one thing you're grateful for
- Use a gratitude app on your phone

To summarize, here are my main points about gratitude:

- Choose to look for gratitude
- Focus on small and specific things to be grateful for
- Continue to find new things to be grateful for
- Find a way to practice gratitude in your life

Making it Your Own

Choosing Gratitude

What are some small and specific things you're grateful for? Below are a few categories to get your thinking started.

I am grateful for this/these:

☐ People in my life_____

☐ Animals in my life_____

☐ Favorite items_____

☐ Activities I enjoy_____

☐ Help I've received_____

☐ Progress I've made_____

☐ Lessons I've learned_____

☐ Other_____

_____

When you think about what you're grateful for, what do you feel?

- Mentally_____

- Physically_____

- Emotionally_____

How could you practice gratitude in your life?

☐ Write in a gratitude journal
☐ Meditate on gratitude
☐ Use a gratitude jar
☐ Share gratitude statements at dinner
☐ Write a letter to a person I'm grateful for
☐ Spend time in nature and look for things to be grateful for
☐ Create a gratitude collage
☐ Set a daily time to be grateful
☐ Use a gratitude app

☐ Other ideas_____

Grateful for Brain Injury?!

You may be on board with the general concept of gratitude I've outlined. Maybe you're even ready to incorporate some of the suggestions. Here's another level of gratitude to consider. Is it possible to be grateful for brain injury itself? My answer is yes. I know, that may seem impossible. Maybe you're even yelling 'No! No! No!' at me right now. If that's where you are, that's ok. It took me many, many years to be grateful for my brain injury.

Remember, finding gratitude doesn't mean that we have to like the situation we're in. We can hate it. I don't like having a brain injury. I would rather that it never happened. However, I've learned that I can <u>both</u> hate the injury itself <u>and</u> be grateful for the good that's come from it.

One of my core beliefs is that all life situations have something to teach us. I've discovered that the way to find gratitude when life is at its worst is to focus on the positives of what I've learned and what I've gained.

Here's how I apply that concept to brain injury:

I can hate my brain injury symptoms, and still be grateful that because of them I've learned how to slow down and pay attention to small joys.

I can dislike what brain injury has done to my life, and still be grateful that it introduced me to many wonderful people I never would have met otherwise.

I can wish my brain injury never happened, and still be grateful that it opened up new passions for me as a brain injury writer, speaker, educator, advocate and peer mentor.

Are you ready to find gratitude within brain injury? If your answer is 'not yet', that's ok. Be patient with yourself and know that this step may be more doable when you're a little further along in your brain injury journey.

If your answer is yes, you can apply the same concepts from general gratitude to gratitude for brain injury.

- Choose to look for gratitude
- Focus on small and specific things to be grateful for
- Continue to find new things to be grateful for
- Find a way to practice gratitude in your life

I know it's not easy to find gratitude within brain injury. It's a long process, but the benefits are well worth it.

Ultimately, gratitude and acceptance have much in common. Both are about acknowledging the devastation of brain injury, and choosing to move forward the best way you can.

Making it Your Own

Grateful for Brain Injury?!

What have you learned or gained because of your brain injury?

☐ Life wisdom_____

☐ New friends_____

☐ New interests_____

☐ Other_____

Fill in the sentences below to create your own brain injury gratitude statements.

Even though I dislike my brain injury, I'm grateful to have learned

_____

_____

Even though I dislike my brain injury, I'm grateful to have gained

_____

_____

Taking it Further

What's one thing you learned from reading this chapter?

_____

_____

_____

What action are you ready to take?

_____

_____

_____

CHAPTER 15

If At First You Don't Succeed, Letting Go May Be What You Need

Some of us think holding on makes us strong,
but sometimes it is letting go.

~Hermann Hesse

Living with brain injury can be a delicate balance between knowing when to try harder and when to just let go and accept what is. Without enough pushing and trying, there won't be any forward progress. Without enough surrendering and letting go, life becomes too full of failure and frustration. Learning to let go is at the heart of accepting brain injury. Each chapter in this book has been building toward this crucial concept.

What do I mean by letting go? Letting go is about being able to acknowledge a situation without resisting it. It's about riding the current of what is, in the moment.

Here's a metaphor to help explain the letting go process. Think of brain injury symptoms like a raging river. You've fallen into that river and are trapped in its swirling waters, struggling to stay afloat. You can see the shore where you used to be and desperately want to get back there. You swim against the current, trying with all your power to return to that shore. That's your only focus. But the river is bigger and stronger than you are; it's out of your control. You can fight and fight and fight, but the shore stays out of reach no matter what you do.

It takes time and a lot of failed attempts, but eventually you realize that you can't get back to your old shore. You know you're stuck in that river and you hate it. So you continue to fight against the current, trying to control something, anything about the experience. However, the river is still more powerful than you are, so you just end up bruised, exhausted and frustrated.

There comes a time when you realize you have to let go—to acknowledge the river's power over you and ride it wherever it's going to take you. There's a freedom that comes from letting go of what you can't control, from surrendering and going with the flow. Even though the ride ahead is still scary and full of challenges, it's the only way forward. Letting go is what can take you toward a new shore.

Making it Your Own

Letting Go—Applying the River Metaphor

Apply the river metaphor to your own brain injury journey. What describes you most right now?

- ☐ Trying to get back to your old shore
- ☐ Fighting the current
- ☐ Going with the flow

If your answer is 'Trying to get back to your old shore', be aware that the information in this chapter could be especially challenging. The concept of letting go may be more than you're ready to process right now. Take your time and know that you can always stop and go back to the earlier chapters of this book. You can't rush your journey. It's about taking in information at a time when it's most helpful for you.

Resistance to Letting Go

It's very common to resist letting go. I struggled mightily with letting go and surrendering to the reality of my brain injury. I hated phrases like 'Let go', 'Give in', 'Surrender', 'Let it be', and 'It is what it is'. In my head, they meant defeat—giving up the fight and waving the white flag on my life. Prior to my brain injury, I'd always lived my life by the motto 'If at first you don't succeed, try, try again'. I believed I could do anything if I worked hard enough at it.

After my car accident, I tried to apply the same philosophy to healing my brain injury. I was not going to give in to it; that seemed like weakness to me. I was going to keep pushing against that river. I believed that trying harder was the only way to keep my head above water.

Every psychologist and counselor I saw told me that Type A, perfectionist, high-achievers like me had a particularly difficult time with letting go. They were right! I believed that if I let go and surrendered to brain injury, my life would be over.

I was wrong in how I thought about letting go. Trying hard is necessary and important, but it's only part of the equation. To reach full acceptance, letting go is also needed. Letting go can move us forward in ways that trying harder can't.

Sometimes people resist letting go because they think it means giving up. That's not true at all. Giving in to brain injury is not giving up on hope, improvement or a happy life. We should never give up on those things.

Making it Your Own

Resistance to Letting Go

What's your reaction to these phrases?

- Let go
- Give in
- Surrender
- Let it be
- It is what it is

_____

_____

_____

_____

_____

Recognizing when it's Time to Let Go

How do you know when it's time to try hard and when it's time to let go? Here are some signs that letting go may be what's needed:

- You're failing over and over again, without any forward progress
- Your strategies aren't working
- You feel stuck
- An activity—or the mere thought of attempting that activity—makes you feel overwhelmed
- The mental, physical or emotional price you pay for an activity outweighs the benefit
- You say the word 'should' a lot: 'I should be able to do this' or 'It shouldn't be like this'
- No matter what you do, the situation can't be changed
- You're resisting the idea of letting go

Making it Your Own

Recognizing when it's Time to Let Go

Which letting go signs do you identify with the most?

- ☐ I'm failing over and over again, without any forward progress
- ☐ My strategies aren't working
- ☐ I feel stuck
- ☐ An activity—or the mere thought of attempting that activity—makes me feel overwhelmed
- ☐ The mental, physical or emotional price I pay for an activity outweighs the benefit
- ☐ I say the word 'should' a lot: 'I should be able to do this' or 'It shouldn't be like this'
- ☐ No matter what I do, the situation can't be changed
- ☐ I'm resisting the idea of letting go

Stages of Letting Go

Letting go is a process that may take a long time. Looking back, I can divide my own letting go process into two stages. First, I had to acknowledge that brain injury changed my life forever. Second, I had to stop resisting my brain injury symptoms. Each of those stages took several years to fully achieve.

Acknowledge the Reality of Brain Injury

From years one through five post-injury, I worked on acknowledging the reality of how brain injury had changed me. Much of that time was spent in denial, as I tried and failed numerous times to return to my old life and my old way of doing things. That's a common pattern for many of us in the early years after brain injury. Our old lives are all we know, so of course we try to get back there.

It took years of failing to convince me that no matter how hard I tried, I wasn't going to make a full recovery from brain injury. No matter how much I pushed, I couldn't go back to my previous life. I wasn't going to get back to my old shore. The old Carole was indeed gone forever. Letting go of those ideas opened the door to creating my new life. That's one of the benefits of letting go. It can create space for a new way of living.

Making it Your Own

Acknowledge the Reality of Brain Injury

On a scale of 1-5, how fully have you acknowledged the reality that brain injury has changed you forever?

1	2	3	4	5
not at all		somewhat		fully acknowledged

What could be holding you back from fully acknowledging that brain injury has changed you forever?

_____

_____

_____

_____

_____

Stop Resisting Brain Injury Symptoms

Acknowledging the reality of my brain injury opened the door to my new life. Between years five and eight post-injury, I concentrated on building that new life. I practiced using strategies to make my life work better. I enjoyed making crafts. I volunteered a few hours a week at the rehab hospital where I'd been an outpatient. I did some speaking about brain injury. I started writing this book. I learned to like myself again.

Although I'd let go of a lot, there was more to do. I'd accepted the reality of my brain injury, but I still thought I could control it. I fought against my symptoms. In particular, I struggled against how unpredictable they were.

I was frustrated by how little it took to overload my brain. I never knew when a sudden noise or movement, flashing lights, too much thinking or too much talking was suddenly going to overwhelm me. I'd learned to carefully plan out my activities using strategies; however, unforeseen circumstances often led to brain overload and the need for family or friends to rescue me. Each overload episode would be followed by days on the couch recovering my mental energy. The emotional fallout from these episodes was equally bad. I felt huge frustration, shame and grief every time they happened.

I believed that I should be able to better control my brain injury symptoms. I'd accepted that I couldn't get rid of them, but I wanted them to behave on my terms. I kept trying to find the right schedule, strategy or treatment that would stop the overloading. I believed that there had to be an answer somewhere 'out there'. In other words, I kept trying harder. Returning to my river metaphor, even though I'd stopped trying to get back to my old shore, I was still resisting the current.

Then, for reasons unknown, I went through a time when I had trouble sleeping. Of course, this left me even more tired and vulnerable to brain overload. As the insomnia continued, I had this thought: *My life is always going to be like this. There will always be some brain injury symptom to deal with, no matter what I do. No matter how hard I try, I cannot change that.*

I'd had that thought before and always pushed it away because it was scary and depressing and I didn't want to believe it. This time, I think the sleep deprivation dulled my natural instinct to ignore the thought and try harder. It broke my usual thought pattern. I didn't have the energy to push any more. Instead, I let the magnitude of those words wash over and through me. I didn't run from their truth; I let it deeply sink in. *My life is always going to be like this. There will always be some brain injury symptom to deal with, no matter what I do. No matter how hard I try, I cannot change that.*

Much to my surprise, I suddenly felt free. It was as if an enormous weight had been lifted from me. I felt lighter inside. On that day, I finally, truly, let go, gave in, surrendered. I stopped fighting what I couldn't control. I switched from struggling against the current to riding with it. I realized I could accept my brain injury symptoms and their unpredictability by just letting them be. The key to acceptance wasn't 'out there' in schedules, strategies or treatments. Rather, it was 'in here', inside me and the way I thought about my brain injury. Letting go was a feeling of victory, not of defeat.

Making it Your Own

Stop Resisting Brain Injury Symptoms

Below is a list of common brain injury symptoms. Place a '✓' next to any symptoms you've accepted and an 'x' next to any symptoms that you resist accepting and fight against.

☐ Memory loss
☐ Mental fatigue
☐ Light sensitivity
☐ Sound sensitivity
☐ Headache
☐ Difficulty concentrating
☐ Difficulty making decisions
☐ Slow thinking
☐ Difficulty reading
☐ Vision changes
☐ Mood swings
☐ Dizziness

☐ Loss of taste/smell
☐ Difficulty planning
☐ Loss of balance
☐ Difficulty initiating tasks
☐ Depression
☐ Loss of sense of self
☐ Anxiety
☐ Overload in busy environments
☐ Speech difficulties

☐ Other_____

☐ Other_____

What's your reaction to this statement? *My life is always going to be like this. There will always be some brain injury symptom to deal with, no matter what I do. No matter how hard I try, I cannot change that.*

_____

_____

Benefits of Letting Go

Letting go can improve life in ways that trying harder doesn't. It can create space for:

- Feelings of peace and serenity
- Increased happiness
- Greater self-acceptance
- Decreased shame about brain injury
- Less emotional suffering when symptoms occur

I know it doesn't seem to make logical sense, but letting go is something that can be a catalyst for moving forward.

Letting go changes nothing and everything both at the same time. Letting go of trying to control my brain injury symptoms didn't change them at all. I still deal with them every single day. My brain fatigues quickly, I overload easily, and sometimes I need to be rescued. I cope with sound, visual and balance sensitivities. I spend more time on my couch resting than I'd like, and sometimes I feel sad about what I can't do. My brain injury symptoms are annoying, time-consuming and limiting. I don't like them.

Letting go does change my relationship to those symptoms. I now treat my brain injury more as a friend, rather than as the enemy who must be destroyed. Instead of fighting against my symptoms, I accept them when they happen and ride the current.

Letting go means I focus on whatever it is I can do in the present moment.

Letting go means I trust that wherever I am right now (even if that place often happens to be resting on my couch) is where I need to be.

Letting go means that even when brain injury symptoms rule my life, I choose to be happy anyway. In fact, since I let go, I've been happier than I was even before my brain injury.

Strategies for Letting Go

Ok, I wonder if any of you are thinking something like this right now: 'There is no way I can let go.' I struggled with that myself for a long time. I remember listening to long-term survivors talk about letting go and accepting brain injury and thinking there was no way I could ever do that. In all honesty, no one was more surprised than me when it happened. Believe that it will be possible for you when you're ready. It takes time for all the pieces to come together. When you've built enough momentum, letting go can happen. Be patient and gentle with yourself.

Or, maybe you're asking something like this: 'But how do I let go?' The letting go process I described may sound kind of like magic. As I've thought more deeply about how letting go happened for me, I've realized that it wasn't instant magic at all. This whole book highlights the journey toward letting go and reaching acceptance. Learning to let go involves talking and listening; acting and reflecting; crying and laughing; asking for and receiving feedback; falling down and getting back up. Like any journey, it's easier with the help of others—family, friends, other brain injury survivors and medical professionals. Momentum toward letting go can build as we do work such as overcoming denial, processing grief, using strategies, building a new life, choosing to laugh, finding silver linings and expressing gratitude.

Everyone's journey toward letting go will be different. My steps will not be the same as your steps. Here are a few pieces of wisdom I've learned from my own journey that may help you in yours:

- *Recognize that everything you're doing right now is part of your letting go journey.* Even if it feels like you're going backward, you are still moving forward.
- *Take your time.* Your pace is your own and no one else's. You can't rush the letting go process.
- *Don't go it alone.* Professional help may be needed to help you work through emotions around letting go and to identify what you may be resisting. Support can also come from family, friends and other brain injury survivors.
- *Regularly do activities that help you stay focused in the present moment.* They're good practice for acknowledging what is and letting go of what can't be controlled. Some examples are mindful breathing, meditation, yoga, Tai Chi, spiritual practice, arts & crafts, music and nature observation.
- *Look at all experience as a teacher.* Try to find something positive to learn from everything that happens to you. That can help you find your own power in situations that are out of your control.

Letting go is a simple idea that's hard to do. It's one of the biggest and most important challenges in reaching acceptance after brain injury. When you can let go and ride the river toward your new shore, you've found your power as a brain injury survivor.

Making it Your Own

Strategies for Letting Go

Below are some of the steps along the path toward letting go. Place a '✓' next to any steps you've already done and an 'x' next to steps that you're working on.

- ☐ I believe letting go can happen for me
- ☐ I am patient and gentle with myself
- ☐ I've learned about my brain injury
- ☐ I've connected with other brain injury survivors
- ☐ I can reflect on and learn from my failures
- ☐ I can acknowledge that brain injury has changed me
- ☐ I ask for help when I need it
- ☐ I listen to suggestions from the people who care about me
- ☐ I use positive self-talk
- ☐ I spend less time comparing the new me to the old me
- ☐ I can recognize and celebrate the progress I've made
- ☐ I've found an activity that the new me can enjoy
- ☐ I'm working through my grief about brain injury
- ☐ I use strategies to get things done
- ☐ I'm building a new life as a brain injury survivor
- ☐ I give to others in ways that I can
- ☐ I've found a way to make meaning out of suffering
- ☐ I can laugh at myself and my brain injury
- ☐ I've found silver linings in my brain injury
- ☐ I can identify things in my life that I'm grateful for
- ☐ I look at all experience as teaching me something
- ☐ I'm moving forward the best way I can

Taking it Further

What's one thing you learned from reading this chapter?

_____

_____

_____

What action are you ready to take?

_____

_____

_____

Conclusion

Never, never, never give up.

~Winston Churchill

Accepting brain injury doesn't happen in days or months. Given the devastating impact of brain injury symptoms, the acceptance process often takes years. The nature of brain injury forces us to give up many of life's joys. As you continue on your personal path to acceptance, here are some things you should never, never, never give up.

Never Give Up on Making Progress

Healing can continue for the rest of your life. It will be slower than you'd like and the gains will be small. However, even small, slow gains can have a positive impact on your life. The progress you make isn't about getting back to the old you, but rather becoming the best new you possible.

Never Give Up on a Meaningful, Happy and Productive Life

Your life may be very different now than you ever imagined. However, when you can let go of your past vision of what you thought life would be, unexpected doors can open. There are many paths to a good life.

Never Give Up on Believing in Yourself

Where you are now is not where you'll be one year, two years, five years or ten years from now. Today's challenges can turn into tomorrow's successes. Believe that you will continue to grow, change and move forward.

Never Give Up on Learning

Brain injury is an ongoing self-education project. There's much to discover about your injury, your new self, your strengths and your challenges. The process may be slow and full of setbacks, but learning is possible. Learning from adversity will increase your resilience.

Never Give Up on Having Dreams

Yes, brain injury often means your dreams have to be revised. However, you can continue to set realistic goals and work toward them at your own pace and in your own time. Dreams for the future encourage you to stretch and push your boundaries.

Never Give Up on Accepting Brain Injury

Your acceptance process is your own and no one else's. It will happen when it's right for you. When you accept what is, you'll be ready to be all you can be as a brain injury survivor.

It's my sincere hope that this book has helped you move forward in your journey as a brain injury survivor. May you root and rise!

Appendix

A List of all the 'Making it Your Own' Workbook Topics and Pages

Acknowledgments

Each of us has cause to think with deep gratitude of those who have lighted the flame within us.

~ Albert Schweitzer

Big thanks go to my amazing writing group: Hilary Zayed, Rorie Lee and Ross Goldberg. They challenged my thinking, helped me to refine my ideas, encouraged me to own my voice as a writer, and cheered me on through the process. They made this book better.

I appreciate the thoughtful suggestions and typo-finding skills of my test readers. Thank you to Mary Starr, Bethany Bryan, Mary Collins, Inga Larson, Annemarie Loffeld and Gail Wormwood.

Graphic designer Kristofor Shisler did great work turning the rough image I created with apps on my phone into cover-worthy art

I'm grateful for the numerous dinner invitations from my friends and neighbors Gordon Shulkin and Diane Chong. They saved me from eating cottage cheese when writing left me too brain-tired to cook.

This book exists because of all that family, friends, fellow survivors and medical professionals did to help me learn to accept brain injury.

Professionals taught me strategies to cope with my challenges, encouraged me as I learned to accept this new life, and have helped me to continue healing. Special thanks to my long-term providers: Lindy Grigel, Homeopathy; Susan Marcet, Social Work; Denise Toppi, Massage Therapy; and Dr. Keelyn Wu, Osteopathy.

New England Rehabilitation Hospital of Portland and Recreation Therapist Kathy Kroll also deserve special thanks. They helped me to build on my strengths and to focus on what I can do. This opened the door to finding purpose in my life as a brain injury survivor.

The people who best understand the brain injury acceptance journey are those who live it. I'm grateful for all I've learned from the WINGS Support Group and from my colleagues in Brain Injury Voices.

There's no way I could have progressed this far without my family and close friends. They have walked this brain injury road with me. They've witnessed my tears, provided rides home, offered caring feedback, and celebrated my successes. With much love, I thank Donald Starr, Mary Starr, Kerem Durdag, Kemal Durdag, Sofia Durdag, Lila Durdag, Sylvia Wallingford and Gail Wormwood.

Lastly, I have to acknowledge two of my greatest influences: my mother, Joyce Starr, and my mentor, Bev Bryant. Sadly, both of them passed away years before I finished *To Root & To Rise*. However, the legacy of what they taught me lives on in these pages, and in my life. I know they would both be proud of what I've accomplished.

If I missed anyone, please accept my apologies and my sincere thanks.

Bibliography

This is a list of books that have inspired me as I learned to accept my brain injury and as I wrote this book. I will be perfectly honest; I have not read every word of all these books. I still struggle with reading due to my brain injury. Some books I did read every word; other ones I skimmed the contents; some I read a few chapters. They're listed here because each in its own way contributed to the person I've become since my brain injury, the way I think, and this book.

Tara Brach, Ph.D., *Radical Acceptance: Embracing your Life with the Heart of a Buddha* (New York: Bantam Books, 2003)

William Bridges, Ph.D., *Transitions: Making Sense of Life's Changes* (Reading, Massachusetts: Perseus Books, 1980)

Beverley Bryant, *In Search of Wings: A Journey Back from Traumatic Brain Injury* (South Paris, ME: Wings Publishing, 1992)

Julia Cameron, *The Artist's Way: A Spiritual Path to Higher Creativity* (New York: Jeremy P. Tarcher/Putnam, 1992)

Pema Chodron, *When Things Fall Apart: Heart Advice for Difficult Times,* (Boulder, CO: Shambhala Publications, 2016)

Gail Denton, Ph.D., *Brainlash: Maximize your Recovery from Mild Traumatic Brain Injury* (New York: Demos Medical Publishing, 1999)

Viktor E. Frankl, M.D., Ph.D., *Man's Search for Meaning,* 4th Edition (Boston: Beacon Press, 2000)

Stephen Joseph, Ph.D., *What Doesn't Kill Us: The New Psychology of Posttraumatic Growth* (New York: Basic Books, 2011)

Andrew Newberg, M.D. & Mark Robert Waldman, *Words Can Change Your Brain* (New York: Plume, 2013)

Janet Niemeier, Ph.D. & Robert Karol, Ph.D., *Overcoming Grief and Loss after Brain Injury* (Oxford: University Press, 2010)

Martin E.P. Seligman, Ph.D., *Flourish: A Visionary New Understanding of Happiness and Well-being* (New York: Atria Paperback, 2013)

Steven M. Southwick, M.D. & Dennis S. Charney, M.D., *Resilience: The Science of Mastering Life's Greatest Challenges* (Cambridge: University Press, 2012)

Barbara Stahura & Susan B. Schuster, M.A., *After Brain Injury: Telling Your Story, A Journaling Workbook* (Wake Forest, NC: Lash & Associates Publishing/Training Inc., 2009)

Diane Roberts Stoler, Ed.D. and Barbara Albers Hill, *Coping with Mild Traumatic Brain Injury* (Garden City Park, NY: Avery Publishing Group, 1998)

Hilary Zayed, *Reinventing Oneself after Loss, An Artful Insight* (Youngsville, NC: Lash & Associates Publishing/Training Inc., 2015)

Index

ABOUT THE AUTHOR

Carole J. Starr has a master's degree in Adult Education. In June of 1999, she was 32 years old, and living a busy life in her home state of Maine. She was building a career as an educator and spent much of her free time playing the violin in a community orchestra and singing soprano in a chorale. She loved to travel and enjoyed spending time with her family and friends.

That life ended in July of 1999, when Carole sustained a brain injury in a car accident. She had to give up her teaching career and her classical music hobby. Carole grieved the loss of her old life and her sense of self. It took her many years to accept her brain injury and the new person she became. She's reinvented herself by focusing on what she can do, one small step at a time.

Carole now delivers inspiring keynote speeches at brain injury conferences. She's also the founder and facilitator of Brain Injury Voices, an award-winning survivor education, advocacy and peer mentoring volunteer group in Maine. She wrote *To Root & To Rise* to share what she's learned about accepting an unexpected new life. Through these activities, Carole has found a new way to be a teacher. She is happy again, even while living with a disability.

Please visit the websites below to contact Carole, watch videos of her keynotes, or learn more about Brain Injury Voices.

CaroleJStarr.com
BrainInjuryVoices.org

Made in the USA
Middletown, DE
30 January 2023

22922586R00126